Nothin' but a Pond Dog

by Llewellyn Emery

ILLUSTRATED BY
Catherine Draycott

THE BERMUDIAN PUBLISHING COMPANY LIMITED

Published by The Bermudian Publishing Company Limited,
P.O. Box HM 283, Hamilton HM AX, Bermuda.

 THE PORTRAYAL OF A SAILOR IN A SHIP'S CROW'S NEST
IS A TRADEMARK OF THE BERMUDIAN PUBLISHING
COMPANY LIMITED

ISBN 976–8143–17–7

Book and cover design by Brimstone Media, Bermuda.
Printed and bound in the U.S.

First Edition February 1996
Reprinted June 1999

PREFACE

The year was 1956. A brash young jelly-legged man, with slick dark hair and looks that made girls swoon, was wailing a Number One Hit Parade song called *Hound Dog*. This teen idol captivated, shocked or bemused millions with outrageous gyrations and fitful spasms that were to become his trademarks. I was more interested in trying to decipher the garbled lyrics of his song that I heard over the radio. If *Hound Dog* contained any innuendo, symbolism or cryptic message, I was, at the naive age of eight, incapable of discerning it. All I knew was, as far as I could figure out, the hound dog about which he sang bore a curious resemblance to my own beloved dog.

I was dumbfounded as I pressed first one ear, then the other, hard against the radio speaker. I strained to catch each phrase as it crackled over the airwaves. The cultures were worlds apart, so how could he sing of sentiments that so closely resembled mine? Jerry Leiber and Mike Stoller may have written *Hound Dog* for Elvis Presley, but it had universal appeal. Millions of people with lovable mutts could identify with the obvious affection this guy felt for his dog. If Leiber and Stoller hadn't written *Hound Dog*, sooner or later someone else might well have written:

> *You ain't nothin' but a Pond Dog*
> *Barkin' all the time.*
> *You ain't nothin' but a Pond Dog*
> *Barkin' all the time.*
> *You ain't never caught a rat.*
> *So you ain't no friend o' mine...*

Who knows? It might have been just as big a hit...

This is no ordinary dog story, however. It is a story about life in an oft-forgotten region of Bermuda, Central Pembroke. The scene is so very different now when I gaze across the cluttered landscape. Today, the average passerby sees an unsightly mountain of crudely-mixed mulch, rubble and garbage in varying stages of decomposition. Debris from the fringes flies about aimlessly under the slightest provocation by the wind. Wild grasses and only the hardiest of vegetation struggle to hide the unsightliness.

In the foreground, impossible to ignore, a swollen mound sprawls imposingly across what used to be lush, green marshlands. Yet we who hail from that area see deep beneath the rotting refuse, where lie the remnants of another life and time. We look back with admitted fondness at the simple pleasures of a world uncomplicated by today's perplexing issues and concerns.

Somewhere between then and now, we created an ecological monster, force-fed with each new day's offering of community garbage. For decades it lay there, its nasty, sore-infested belly heaving and swelling as it gulped its daily fare. The more garbage we produced, the more it consumed. We watched helplessly as it grew out of control. The monster refused to die.

Ultimately, we had little choice but to bury it alive and wait for its demise.

It's hard to believe that fond memories could lie buried beneath such ugliness, but Pembroke Marsh was not always so grotesque, nor will it always be. The plan, already well under way, is to build a vast new park. A Herculean challenge awaits those whose job that will be. In the meantime, as the closure of the dump heralds the end of an era, I prefer to remember the region for what it used to be, a poor area rich in culture, and the playground of lowly Pond Dogs.

We who grew up in those environs have a special empathy for Pond Dogs. Like them, we too were often stereotyped, written off as "amounting to nothing," shooed away as "undesirables," judged by mere outward appearance or geographic origins. Were we not just simple folk from 'back o' tahn?' Surely we couldn't be proficient at anything but the menial and the mundane.

The term 'Pond Dog' eventually became a euphemism for anyone living in the immediate environs of The Pond. And since Pond Dogs are natural scavengers, people who came in search of 'treasure' amid the trash heaps also earned that label.

We're not offended by that designation. On the contrary, today we use the expression just as teasingly and affectionately when referring to ourselves as we do when speaking of the likes of Barker, my real-life childhood Pond Dog. Thus, there are Pond Dogs ranging from the famous to the not-so-famous to the downright infamous. Some are professionals, others are labourers. Some princes, others paupers. Nevertheless, there are three common threads which bind us—our cultural heritage, the area in which we grew up, and the memories that we share.

We know better than to look down on Pond Dogs. For us, they are a living metaphor.

1

The Pond

Barker was what we used to call a 'Pond Dog.' He was born and abandoned amid the reeds on the northeast fringe of The Pond. That's where 'Uncle' Albert, a friend of the family, found the litter of four.

It wasn't unusual for someone to find newborn pups in the marsh. In those days, dogs roamed the area at will. Some of these dogs were renegade household pets who had answered the call of the wild. Others had been deliberately taken there and abandoned by their wretched owners. Still others were born there 'in the wild.' All of these we called Pond Dogs (the nearest U.S. equivalent would probably be junk-yard dogs).

Whenever someone found a litter of pups, they'd take them home and try to find homes for them among families who lived nearby. Eventually, any dog bred within view of The Pond was considered a Pond Dog, too (and probably did have at least a trace of Pond Dog in it).

Since The Pond provides the backdrop for all that will unfold henceforth, you must first know something about the geography of the area in which this story finds its setting.

Years ago in Bermuda, the Pembroke Marsh area hosted more than just the Island's garbage dump. The dump area was flanked by several acres of thick, jungle-like greenery, the densest part of which we called The Jungle. Cliff Looby, playing the role of Tarzan, once used it as a movie set, I vaguely recall.

Right next door, east of The Jungle, was a barren, gravelly patch of ground, which was absolutely flat. It was perfect for softball games, because there were no windows within range of even the best-hit ball, be it fair or foul. We called this curious, bleached tract of parched land The Desert.

Way west of The Desert, The Jungle and the dump, and tucked away amid the tall reeds, was a tiny, landlocked body of water. It was visible only from surrounding higher elevations,

and perfectly reflected the cobalt sky. According to neighbourhood legend, it was bottomless, fed via underground passageways connecting it to the ocean. I remember grown-ups forbidding us to go there. They said if someone drowned there, his body would disappear. Allegedly, the bloated corpse would eventually surface near The Ducking Stool on North Shore, about a half-mile away. The sheer horror of such a prospect was enough to deter any neighbourhood child who might otherwise be tempted to sneak out for a swim. Every child on the planet knew better than to trespass upon that forbidden territory.

We called this little, isolated body of blue The Lake.

Along the entire southern boundary of the marsh ran the Pembroke Canal. This was, indeed, connected to the ocean. That its levels coincided with high and low tides confirmed the theory (So perhaps the aforementioned story about The Lake was true after all). A glorious oleander hedge ran the length of the canal's southern bank, neatly camouflaging the entire waterway. Convenient breaks in the hedgerow marked suitable points for crossing. As the name 'canal' implies, it was a narrow aqueduct. It channelled brackish water to an unknown destination for an unknown purpose. Of course, its purpose was not unknown to every child who lived in the vicinity, or whoever attended the adjacent Central School. We knew instinctively why it was there.

It was there for us to attempt to cross via the narrow, unsteady plank that spanned its width. It was there for us to fall into should our feebler attempts fail, or some prankster thwart our efforts. Many a daring child tried to jump across, broad jump style, and suffered the penalty for failure. So clearly, the serpentine canal was there to lure us, to dare us, to egg us on. Then it could humiliate us and earn for us a sound licking when we arrived home covered with pond scum.

It was a perpetual source of tadpoles, mullets, and champion frogs. At any given time, a small band of adventurous boys could organise a nail-biting swimming race, each boy shouting and waving to urge his chosen frog to victory.

It was a place into which we could toss a rock, and admire the splash it created. The splash was all the more admirable if it soaked some 'innocent' bystander, who was sure to 'get licks' just for being somewhere his parents forbade him to be. That canal was there to make us disobey our parents, and to teach us, the hard way, the consequences of disobedience. Every child who ever ventured there knew that.

We called this alluring, meandering canal The Ditch. We also called it The Pond. Actually, we called everything associated with that area The Pond. For example, sometimes, we spoke of the dump as The Pond. (Some people said "Trash Pond" for clarification, although purists rejected that expression as redundant.) At other times, we referred to the entire marshland by that name. In fact, The Pond dominated that part of the parish so much that people thought of the immediate neighbourhood as The Pond, too. Even Parson's Road, which bypasses the marsh to the south, was unofficially, but popularly known as Pond Road. It used to provide vehicular access to the dump via Blyden's Corner, but that was before the road was re-routed. The portion of Glebe Road which borders The Pond area on the east side is still known as Pond Hill.

We all knew which definition of The Pond applied by the context in which it was used. Thus, a trip to The Pond to get baby-carriage wheels, or box wood, or bicycle parts, obviously meant that we were going to the dump section. A search through The Pond for pond-sticks would take you through the mucky marsh where the reeds grew. Falling into, jumping, or crossing The Pond could only apply to The Ditch. Whereas giving The Pond as your home address clearly meant you lived somewhere on Parson's Road, or nearby.

To illustrate the extent to which our world revolved around that area, even a trip overseas was jokingly referred to (in the vernacular) as "goin' 'cross de puhwn." In our own interpretation of the saying, The Pond expanded to become the entire Atlantic Ocean, the ultimate Pond. Similarly, tuning your radio dial to a foreign station was called "goin' 'cross de puhwn." A radio's worth was often measured by whether or not it could reach across the ocean in the daytime.

Pond dogs could run wild and thrive in this sprawling, swampy reserve. After all, there was an endless supply of food from the dump. Hotels, restaurants, bakeries, grocery stores and households all disposed of garbage there. Discarded crates, cardboard boxes, and derelict vehicles made excellent shelters. Water oozed from the sodden ground, or settled in pools, unable to drain or soak away after a heavy rain. A marauding band of thirsty dogs could drink their fill, then wallow through the rest in wasteful revelry. A healthy rat population provided sport for any dog who fancied the thrill of the hunt. In view of the size of some of those pond rats, though, I sometimes wondered who were the hunters and who the hunted.

2

Portrait
of a
Pond Dog

I was about five years old and living on the outskirts of the City of Hamilton—just out of range of The Pond. One day, Uncle Albert presented us with two of the pups he'd rescued.

They were adorable, of course. What self-respecting five-year-old boy wouldn't find any kind of puppy adorable? They were both golden brown with patches of white on their chests. One had more white than the other. I recall arbitrarily claiming the one with more brown, a male, as mine. My two sisters could share the other one.

The house we lived in was atop Parker's Hill. The vast hill-top was devoid of any houses beyond ours, so the entire area became our extended yard. Neighbourhood children energetic enough to make the climb to the top could laugh, play, scream, and fly their kites without disturbing a soul.

We could hardly wait for our pups to grow big enough to be allowed to romp with us. As it turned out, they never did grow very big. They started off full of promise, but I guess the big dog genes just weren't there.

We noticed that my dog was very alert and that he barked

incessantly, so there was little agonising over what to name him. I've forgotten what we named the other one. Not that it matters much, for the poor thing contracted some dreadful disease, like rabies, or distemper, and had to be put down.

The horrifying thing was the Dogcatcher Guy showed up in the yard with a sack in his hand and announced (we kids thought rather callously) the dog would have to be put down. By my childish reckoning, however, he didn't say "put down." He said "shot!" He took (or chased) the poor little critter out into the field, out of sight of our yard. Then, again according to my probably distorted but, I think, lucid five-year-old's impression, he shot the dog. Surely it couldn't be a figment of my boyish imagination. A shot rang out, and that evil man returned with the lifeless carcass of our beloved pet, in that bag of his. We hated that faceless, nameless man.

At least we still had Barker. We agreed he'd be the family's dog. Secretly, though, I knew he was mine. "A boy and his dog…" Had not the story been related a billion times, at least? Whoever heard of "a boy, his two sisters, his mom, his dad and their dog?" Clearly he was mine. I would, in my magnanimous spirit, share him with the others, of course.

Barker loved his early growing-up days in the remote, open space of Parker's Hill. They were delightful days for our family, too. If we had stayed there much longer, I'm sure we would have become either recluses or one of the fittest families around. Instead, after about three years, we moved 'round The Pond, not a mile away.

We were only a stone's throw from the Poor House, a symbolism which was wasted on me at the time. The place was later rebuilt and more appropriately renamed The Pembroke Rest Home. Suddenly, though, everything about our new locale was different—even the climate. Perhaps it was the change in altitude.

Hot, dusty summers, and bone-chilling, damp winters— that's my earliest recollection of life on Pond Road. We waged an incessant battle against the dust in the summer, because of the location of the house. The window blinds were caked with a film of dust, no matter how often we cleaned them. The front door was almost never opened, lest the dust stirred up by passing traffic find its way indoors, which it did eventually, anyhow.

But as intrusive and all-pervasive as the dust was, I would to this day prefer it to the dampness. Br-r-r-r! That dampness got into your bones, your joints, your marrow. Creeping, sneaky fingers that crawled into your house through every crack, tickled your ears and neck, and sent chills down your spine. And, when every crack was sealed (as if that were possible) it came through the walls, leaving them so cold and clammy, the best paint couldn't stick to them. It took a long, hot summer to drive the dampness out of those walls, but that only meant we were in for an even damper winter.

Unrelenting dampness oozed its way up through the floorboards, and into the soles of your feet, numbing your toes. It permeated the air and seeped into your shoulders and back. It crept into your bed, turning the steel spokes of the headboard into icicles, and leaving the bed sheets moist and uninviting.

That dampness, inventor of its own cruel twist to the Midas touch by turning to cold everything it touched, enveloped you. There remains to this day no defence against it.

The house we'd call home for the next five years or so, was right smack on Parson's Road. The asphalt of Parson's Road was our front yard. Our front door and window blinds swung out into the street. There wasn't so much as a sidewalk between us and the traffic. Gone were the rolling, grassy knolls and hiding places, the trees and bushes, the breathtaking climb to the seclusion of the hilltop. Now, our backyard consisted of three patches of concrete, two at street level on the east and west ends, the other, elevated and a little further to the south. The latter was accessible via a flight of concrete steps. Neither tree, shrub, nor blade of grass graced our new yard.

Worse yet, now there were neighbours above, behind, beside, and across the street from us. Barker would have to be tied.

"It's for his own good," we were assured. Otherwise, he might run out into the street and be squashed by a car; chase after somebody on a bike and bite them; get into fights with neighbourhood hoodlum dogs; wander into someone else's yard; bite some bratty child who teased him; bite the postman; bite the metreman; bite the grocery-boy—all distinct possibilities, I admit.

So, the rule was that poor Barker had to remain chained to a stake in the yard.

We assigned him the upper yard. From there, he barked at every strange sound and every real or imagined passerby. Sometimes, I believe, he barked at nothing at all. Or perhaps it was at everything—the concrete, the traffic, the sheer frustration and oppression of his chains; the loss of Parker's Hill which was subsequently bulldozed into flat oblivion.

He had a doghouse to shelter him from the elements, but elected not to use it. Pond dogs are like that, you know. I used to think he was just trying to show us how tough he was, that when we were not looking he retreated to the shelter which he only pretended to scorn. Or, was he trying to get our sympathy, playing some kind of mind-game, a war of wills? We would be inside, all "comfy and cozy," drinking hot cocoa, kerosene heater blazing, while he lay huddled in a pathetic little ball, quivering, whimpering, dying for the comfort of indoors. Did he want us to feel guilty? If so, we never did.

Barker never spent a day of his life indoors. Dogs belonged outside. Besides, he was nothing but a Pond Dog. Pond Dogs were inherently tough, a durable breed, unaccustomed and ill-suited to the indoors.

We fed him once a day. He ate with such gusto, the food was nearly gone before we could retreat down the steps. No matter what we fed him (and we did feed him some rather disgusting-looking things at times), he was always so appreciative. I never knew him to turn his nose up at anything set before him. Often, he ate what we didn't, wouldn't, or couldn't eat—which wasn't much, now that I think about it. So, we had to supplement our sparse table scraps with store-bought dogfood.

I can remember feeling repulsed by the appearance and smell of that stuff, as I dished it out of the can. It just sat there, particles of unrecognisable gunk, moulded into the shape of the can, each 'flavour' looking and smelling the same—putrid. I'd add warm water to the packaged, dry dog food to soften those little, rock-hard pellets and make them swell in the dish to yield double or triple the amount. All the while, I'd feel ashamed for feeding it to him. But good ol' Barker would just wolf it down and look for more, wagging his tail gratefully, erasing my feelings of guilt and easing my troubled conscience. Pond Dogs are like that. They'll eat anything—and be grateful for it.

For example, I hated those cooked cereals like Cream of Wheat, Quaker Oats, Corn Meal Mush, porridges of any kind. Despite all creative attempts by Mom to disguise them (sugar, cinnamon, butter, raisins, honey), nothing could enhance them enough for me to like them. As far as I was concerned, she could dress them up with glasses and a fake nose and moustache. I'd still recognise them for what they were—despicable, unfit for human consumption.

But Barker loved them. That only reinforced my low opinion of their worth. Can you imagine? I endured marathon stand-offs at the table. I defied every threat, coaxing, and cajoling. I resisted every ultimatum, even risked solitary confinement, rather than succumb and actually swallow any of that horrid stuff. Then, after the gruel had coagulated and further deteriorated into something worthy only of burial as hazardous waste, Barker would eat it. Whatever was served him, he ate—even chicken bones.

I was well past the age of twenty when I first heard someone say, with all seriousness, that you should never feed chicken bones to a dog. They said a dog could be killed by eating chicken bones. I laughed. This was a revelation to me. Barker had eaten thousands of the things. It was a real treat to get a pile of chicken bones to eat.

The only way I could imagine a dog dying from eating chicken bones, was if he was doing so in the middle of the road and didn't get out of the way before the truck ran over him (cause of death: Eating chicken bones). Every Pond Dog I ever knew ate chicken bones (if they should ever be fortunate enough to find any). I dare say, I knew of some who ate whole, live chickens, with nothing left to show for it but some feathers. Just ask some of the many neighbours who kept a few fowls in the yard.

There's another incident to support my contention that a Pond Dog will eat anything. Bear in mind that these were the days when you could pass by almost any home on a Sunday, and smell the unmistakable aroma of a leg of lamb roasting in the oven. Now, even the leanest leg of lamb yielded a substantial pool of grease, which solidified into a whitish, marble-like slab, but with the texture of lard, and of course, the aroma of roasted lamb. Most people spooned off as much of this heavy grease as they could before making gravy from the remaining drippings.

The dear old lady whose yard overlooked ours must have saved up about twenty-five Sundays'-worth of this grease of lamb. I prefer to think she intended it to be a special treat for Barker. Any other motive for what she did would be too sinister to contemplate. At an opportune moment, when none of our family was around, she presented him with a large roasting pan full of congealed lamb fat. The slab was nearly three inches thick.

We didn't see him, but Barker was probably delirious with joy when he sniffed at that suspicious-looking hunk of grease and discovered it gave off the same, unmistakable aroma that had tortured him every Sunday as it wafted through the neighbourhood. Leg of lamb! How he must have rejoiced as he sunk his teeth into it. He must have chomped at it again and again and again, until he could eat no more. Then, because there was still more and he was unaccustomed to leaving anything on his plate, in true Pond Dog tradition, he tried to finish it.

That's how I learned what the expression "as sick as a dog" means. I saw it graphically illustrated that day, all over our yard.

When we found him, he looked pitiful, apologetic and confused. He was trying to figure out: How could something smell so much like meat, and not be meat? Poor Barker wasn't himself for several days thereafter, but he bounced back, as Pond Dogs always do.

I was to see that pathetic look again. It seems that Barker had adopted as his motto: If it moves, bite it! If it doesn't move, eat it! Living as close to The Pond as we did meant that "things that moved" frequently found their way into our yard. Whether seeking a better life, satisfying their curiosity, searching for adventure, foraging for food, or purely by accident, rats and frogs were regular, unwelcome visitors. These were no ordinary rats, but enormous, over-sized rodents that shuffled because they were too big to scamper.

Likewise, some of the frogs were so huge, they had to lumber rather than leap. Barker went berserk at the mere sight of one of these intruders. He definitely gave us the impression that if he ever caught one of them, well, let's just say it would not be a pretty sight. The day he finally got hold of a frog was unforgettable.

Bermuda's frogs, I'm told, are really toads, introduced back in the late 1800s by Captain Nathaniel Vesey. They proliferated to such an extent, they've been completely integrated into our culture. The dwindling numbers of their modern-day descendants now enjoy full Bermudian status. (Although we never disputed their correct name, however, Pond Dog tradition insisted on calling them frogs, political correctness notwithstanding.) Having personally observed the marvellous processes by which the egg, the tadpoles, then the baby frogs develop, and in such staggering numbers, I'm not surprised the population has thrived. This is certainly no small accomplishment when we consider lowly frogs are defenceless against man and the motor car. However, they aren't entirely defenceless against beasts—dogs, for example.

Pond Dogs like Barker spent a good portion of their days taunting and threatening frogs, yearning for the opportunity to bite into one. On the other hand, the more experienced dogs always stopped short of the final assault.

They knew better than to bite a frog. You see, a frog has two poison sacs at the back of its head, right where its shoulders would be (if a frog had a neck and shoulders). When threatened, it'll puff up like a balloon, so those two sacs become prominent. Its body also becomes so wide the narrowest place for a predator to grab it is near the head, right where the poison sacs are located At the same time, it secretes a slimy fluid through its leathery skin.

Pond frogs, great big ones, paraded past Barker, just out of reach of his chain. Often, they'd nestle in holes in the wall nearby, and stare out at him, a deliberate act of provocation. They usually came out at night or on rainy days, and when they did they drove him wild. We could hear the frustration in his bark as he yanked at his tether and ran back and forth, wishing to be free. Surely, it was during such moments of exasperation that he reaffirmed his oath, namely to catch one of his tormentors one day. And pity the frog that happened to have the misfortune of being the one he caught. It would not be a pretty sight.

Indeed, it wasn't. We found poor Barker sprawled in the yard, foaming at the mouth, his tongue hanging out, eyes closed, sides heaving in laboured breath. He'd finally succeeded in the realisation of his dream—to bite into one of those frogs, and the frog won. Nobody had told poor Barker about the secret weapon. We thought he knew. Wasn't he a Pond Dog?

Whatever happened to instinct? The problem was that he lacked field experience. Now he lay there poisoned, and we kids knew he was going to die.

Mom rushed to the rescue. Those were the days when parents knew exactly what to do in every crisis. They had an instinctive knowledge of home remedies for every imaginable emergency, and a few unimaginable ones, too—like frog-biting, for example. What medical book would tell you: "Here's what to do if your dog ever bites a frog?" She washed his mouth out with diluted vinegar, cleaned off his dangling tongue and put it back where it belonged, then gave him milk to drink. This time he really was sick (as you know what), but Mom had saved his life. He looked appropriately embarrassed and apologetic, but thankful to be alive.

You might think that thenceforth Barker kept a safe distance from frogs. Not so. He still pursued them relentlessly—snarling, threatening, longing to get a hold of another (or the same) one, so he could do it right. He never did get it right. Some time later, we were going through the same scenario, the foaming at the mouth, the vinegar, the milk.

We never found any dead or wounded frogs, though.

The problem with Barker was really one of pedigree, or rather, lack of it. He was nothing but a mongrel Pond Dog. No self-respecting dog of pedigree would want to bite an ugly frog. Barker was living proof that "you can take the dog out of The Pond, but you can't take The Pond out of the dog." There was something in his lovable nature that connected irresistibly with The Pond and things of The Pond.

Take, for example, his occasional excursions. In something comparable to a Houdini escape act, Barker would manage to get loose from his tether. How he did it mystifies me to this day. Of course, whenever he made a successful break, there was no doubt about where he would go. After all, The Pond was just across the street, a stone's throw away. It was the only truly open space in the area. Besides, it was where his roots were.

We always knew exactly where he had been, and what he had been doing. His lower body would be soaking wet and caked in muck from cavorting through The Pond. Clearly, he had gone for a swim, and romped about with his pals to his heart's content. It was as if he just needed that Pond 'fix' once in a while.

I wish I could have seen him in those moments of abandon. What a treat it would have been to see him enjoying himself so utterly. When he'd had enough, he returned, acting as if nothing was amiss, convinced we couldn't see (or smell) the physical evidence of where he had been.

We scolded him every time, but we also understood. It was

the call of the wild, or, more precisely, the call of The Pond, he was answering. And he was not alone. Scores of his domesticated peers also sneaked away to rendezvous in packs for an occasional fling. They caroused through the reedy marshlands, galloped across The Desert, wallowed in the mud and peat moss. They did battle in The Jungle, swam in the stagnating Pond waters, rummaged through the garbage heaps, and dined on tainted food scraps. For them, it was the life of Riley, a respite from the boredom of endless confinement in someone's back yard. Mongrels of all descriptions drank their fill of this good life before returning, rejuvenated, to their mundane duties as household pets.

Some couldn't tear themselves away from this glorious freedom, this life of abandon. They elected to stay and to seek acceptance into a pack as permanent residents. These, and any subsequent offspring, became true renegades, the marauders, whose reputations were often mistakenly attached to the groups of 'innocent' part-time revellers. Their vicious, dog-eat-dog, survival-of-the-fittest behaviour gave Pond Dogs a bad name.

"I know. Maybe Barker's trying to tell us he'd like to go swimming with us," I suggested in his defence one day.

"Let's take him with us for a swim—in real water—in the ocean. Wouldn't he love that!"

The idea was that once he had experienced the exhilaration of an ocean swim at our favourite spot, he'd never want to swim in that yucky Pond again.

We started off on the long, hot trek to Deep Bay, two miles away. Barker led the way, straining at his chain with typical exuberance. That was fine for him. He didn't have to carry anything. We had to carry the blanket, towels, inner-tube, mask, flippers, sandwiches, drink—and control him, all while wearing flip-flops.

How does he know the way? I wondered, the first time we took him. The salty scent of the ocean and visions of us plunging into those inviting, blue-green waters urged us on.

Finally, we reached the top of the steps leading down to the cove. We released Barker from his chain and watched him scamper down the steps and into the water. He barked excitedly as if to say: "Come on in. The water's fine."

"Look! He's doing the dog paddle," my baby sister said.

"Hey, Mom. How come Barker knows how to swim and this is only his first time in the sea?"

"He's been practising in The Pond," I said.

"Dogs just naturally know how to swim," Mom explained. "They're born knowing how to. It's called instinct."

"In stink?" I joked, and we all giggled.

The sound of his barking echoed off the cliffs of Deep Bay. He must have liked the special effects because he never stopped barking the whole time we were there. We laughed at first, but after two hours we'd had enough.

"It's a good thing we had the cove all to ourselves today," said my older sister as Barker led us homeward. "This stupid dog would have gotten on everyone's nerves."

"Don't call my dog stupid."

"He is stupid."

"No, he isn't. You're stupid."

"All right, you two. Cut it out."

"Yes, Mom."

"Stupid dog," she whispered.

"Just like you," I whispered back.

The walk home felt longer than the first leg of the journey. A Hillman convertible taxi with a fringed top came cruising toward us.

"Can we catch a taxi?"

"You can't take a dog in a taxi."

"Yes, you can."

"No, you can't."

"Who asked you?"

We walked all the way home.

Barker had splashed around with us obligingly and patronised us. He seemed to enjoy himself and I think he was grateful we included him. But, he couldn't wait to wash off that salt with another good Pond swim!

When I reached the age of nine, I was considered capable and responsible enough to take Barker out on the street alone. There was no special leash for walking him. I had to use his long, cumbersome chain as a leash. Barker was so eager and excited when he sensed he was about to be taken for a walk, he was nearly uncontrollable. First, he leaped about deliriously and ran circles around me, wrapping the chain around my legs and bruising my shins. Meanwhile, I tried to release the chain from the stake, and to remain standing. Then he raced off toward the steps leading to the lower yard, dragging me along with him. I struggled to keep this bull under control. Knowing I had to shorten the chain, I gathered in the surplus, and held that in one hand, while 'El Torro' strained eagerly at the other end.

Once we had reached the roadside, he changed gears. Finding new strength, he raced off in whichever direction he wanted to go, forcing me to run to keep up with him. He always insisted on setting the pace, and I fought to slow him down. We never went for walks. We just fought the whole time for control, with Barker always emerging as the winner. I still remember that ill-fated summer day, when I made a grave and costly mistake.

"Going barefooted" was a symbol of freedom of a sort—freedom from school and uniforms, freedom from rules, freedom from convention. Summer provided the perfect opportunity to go barefooted. You haven't lived until you've spent an entire summer running barefooted, enduring the searing heat of the asphalt roads, the prickly feeling of tiny pebbles under foot.

There's nothing like the feel of hot sand, warm mud, or wet grass on the soles of your liberated feet. And there's an indescribable euphoria that accompanies each barefooted splash in a puddle of water after a summer rain.

By the end of summer, when you no longer have to step gingerly over even the most hostile terrain, because your soles are well calloused and impervious to pain, you feel invincible.

I was barefooted when we ventured out of our gate and onto Parson's Road on that hapless summer day. Barker was leaning forward, straining like a husky pulling a heavy sled—his signal that he wanted to run. So, we ran. Well, I ran—Barker galloped. When he bolted, he dragged me off balance, causing me to stumble. As I tried to keep up with him and regain my balance, I stubbed the fleshiest part of my right big toe on the coarse road surface.

The pain was instant and excruciating. My toe split open, spouting blood profusely. Barker was unaware of my crippled state. He was still intent on reaching the other end of Parson's Road in record time. Needless to say, he had a very short 'walk' that day. I had to struggle to haul him in, before hobbling back home for medical attention. My toe and my summer were ruined.

While languishing at home waiting for my toe to heal, soaking my foot in warm water and Epsom salts, watching new flesh form, and marvelling at the gradual emergence of a new toenail, I vowed never to take Barker for a walk again with my feet unshod. They would have to remain soft, pink and tender through the rest of that summer holiday. Invincibility would have to be postponed 'til the following year.

3

Errands and museums

Under the pressure of my constant pleadings, and finally confident that we would act responsibly and not become a couple of neighbourhood hooligans if allowed to venture out of the yard with Barker untethered, Mom and Dad gradually eased the rules of confinement to the yard. They even began to send us on errands.

"I want you to go to the store and get me a can of Hunt's tomato sauce," Mom said one day. "Not tomato paste—tomato sauce."

"Yes, Mom. Can I take Barker?"

"Yes, but hurry back. I need that tomato sauce right away. Take two-and-six off my dresser."

"If there's enough change left, can I buy a Dixie Cup?"

"In that case, take an extra shilling and get Dixie Cups for your sisters, too."

There used to be a small field on the corner of Parson's and Glebe where the playground is now. Some of the boys were about to start a football game there with a real football. Sometimes we just kicked an empty tin about, or perhaps a tennis ball, but this was special.

"Hey Llew, we just got de ball pumped up an' wah havin' a li'l kick. Wanna be goalie?"

"Na-ah, I have to run an errand for my momma."

"C'mon, bie. Jus' for a li'l while."

"Yah, c'mon Llew. We need a goalie."

How could a lad resist?

I wasn't sure if Barker was cheering my goalkeeping heroics every time I got possession of the ball, or trying to remind me about our errand, but finally, after nearly an hour, I heeded his remonstrations and tore myself away. We ran the rest of the distance to the store. I wondered if Mom would notice how long we took. I needed a plausible excuse. *Let's see. I had to go to three different stores trying to find it? Nope, that won't work. I know—I can say Barker ran off and I couldn't find him. No, poor Barker—I can't blame him for my mistake. I'd better just tell the truth.*

Mr. Phipps' store was a museum. In fact, it was one of at least a dozen quaint little neighbourhood convenience stores sprinkled within a mile radius of The Pond. Each one was unique yet uncannily similar. After a while you got to know which store was most likely to meet a particular, vital need. For example, some refunded you the sixpence deposit for each empty mineral bottle returned, guaranteeing you ready cash, while others accepted empties only in exchange for the purchase of another bottle of mineral. Some gave you more candies for a penny than others. Some sold ice-cream by the scoop, whereas others sold only Dixie Cups, Bearhugs and Popsicles. Some stocked dog food, some didn't.

"Wait here, Barker." Dogs were not allowed inside.

There were shelves from floor to ceiling. Anything ever put into a can or jar could be found within arm's reach on the well-stocked lower shelves of that cramped little shop. Higher up were all things ever put into boxes. Above the packaged items near the ceiling were paper products.

Items in the latter two categories old Mr. Phipps retrieved by hooking them with a broomstick that had a nail driven through one end. He'd pull them off the shelf and catch them with such casual ease that he earned my undying admiration. I didn't think old people could catch, or that they'd even be interested.

The chin-high counter was decorated with huge jars of assorted candy, a giant roll of brown paper, a large spool of twine, and a scale with a set of brass weights. Behind the counter was a table with a machine for slicing ham. There was also another huge roll of semi-transparent wrapping paper. I noticed that he always wrapped ham and codfish in the light paper first—never the brown—and wondered why. Under the table were sacks of flour, potatoes and more. Through a glass panel in the front of the counter I could see Juicy Fruit, Double Mint and Spearmint Gum, and every kind of chocolate bar the world had ever conceived.

I was right in the middle of day-dreaming about buying one of every chocolate, biscuit, and candy in the store, when Mr. Phipps' voice intruded.

"What can I do for you, young man?"

"Good afternoon, Mr. Phipps." Suddenly my mind went blank.

"Uh-h, I'd like to have three Dixie Cups, please." Then, the friendly red family of Hunt's products on the shelf caught my eye. There was tomato sauce, stewed tomatoes, tomato paste... "Oh, and a tin of Hunt's tomato paste, please," I said, relieved and proud that my memory hadn't failed me after all.

Outside, Barker was waiting patiently to escort me back home to meet my doom on two counts. It wasn't that I was forgetful. I was confused. I had the same problem with baking soda versus baking powder, and codfish versus dumbfish. Why do they make the names so similar, I wondered.

And why do parents insist on emphasising what not to get. It was the power of suggestion, like telling someone not to think about a pink elephant. I spent a lot of time and energy running back to the store to exchange things. Of course, Mom wanted to write everything down on a piece of paper for me to hand to the grocer, but I protested that would be too humiliating. After all, I was a big boy, wasn't I?

There was another errand Barker and I delighted to run. When Mom cooked supper she often prepared an extra plate. She carefully covered it with waxed paper, then wrapped it in a towel to keep it hot. Then she slid it into a brown paper bag along with eating utensils and a dinner napkin, folded the open end of the bag under and placed it in my extended hands just so.

"Be careful. Take your time. And don't forget, wait for her to finish so that you can bring back the dirty dishes." I knew the procedure well but another gentle reminder didn't hurt.

Barker knew the way up the winding path and across the bank to the steps of the ramshackle old house where the indigent but kindly old lady lived. She was a dear friend of Mom's. We called her 'Sister' Simons.

"Good evenin', Sister Simons. I brought you some supper," I'd call out through the peeling paint on the back door.

"Come in," a tiny, frail voice would respond. Barker knew that meant me but not him. He'd slump on the doorstep and snooze while I continued my mission.

"My momma sent you something to eat." I'd set the bag down and, carefully removing the contents, I'd prepare her table. She was always so grateful.

"You came all the way up here by yourself?" she'd ask.

"No, I came with my dog. He's waiting outside."

"You can bring him in. I don't mind."

"Oh, that's okay. He's used to being outside."

It was always dark inside the old tin-roofed house. She seemed to like it that way. Thick floral drapes covered the windows. A stifling scent of liniment clung to the stale air, threatening to overpower me. I'd leave the top half of the kitchen door ajar to allow more light to filter through and to improve the ventilation.

Everything inside was old and most of it untouched for at least a decade. I was never bored while waiting for her to eat, though I don't know if I can speak for Barker. I had scores of fascinating items to distract me. There were hats she used to wear, faded gloves and musty clothes. A large porcelain pitcher and matching basin with ornate artwork sat on the sideboard. Then there was the organ. My fingers itched to touch it to see if it worked. Summoning the nerve I asked, "Does this organ work, Sister Simons?"

"Some of the keys still work. Try it." I sat before the contraption, stretching my short legs and tiptoeing to reach the pedals. As I pumped the pedal, pulled at knobs indiscriminately, and poked the keys at random, the old organ responded with marvellous hoarse tones which convinced me I was a budding musician.

Sometimes I looked at her old books and she talked to me about what paradise was going to be like, and about how much she was looking forward to being there. An errand to old Sister Simons' house was never a chore. It was a mission of mercy, a learning experience, and a visit to a museum the likes of which few will ever experience.

4

Submarines and laundry

There wasn't much for a boy and his dog to do back then, so we had to invent our own amusement. Barker would try to bite flies out of mid air. We called them Pond flies. Every once in a while, he'd lunge forward and snap his jaws, all in one motion. I can't imagine he actually wanted to eat those disgusting Pond flies, although, if he happened to catch one, I doubt if he would have let it go.

As I watched, my mind searched for theories to explain such beastly behaviour. One: He was doing it to keep from getting bored. Two: He was just practising. You know, keeping his reflexes sharp. Three: These miserable flies were so irritating they provoked him to the point of desperation. Four: He was just a Pond Dog living up to his creed: "If it moves, bite it."

Mom had a sheltered laundry area in the lower yard, out back. Sometimes we watched her doing the laundry. She did it the hard way, not automated-style. If I watched long enough, she'd give me something to do, which was really great, because then I'd get to play in the water when she left me to carry out her instructions. What better amusement could there be than

that? I even made it a point to carry in my pocket my little two-inch plastic, baking soda-propelled submarine that came as the prize in a box of Rice Krispies.

Submarine test dives required large bodies of water. Heretofore, my experiments had been limited to either the rather cramped confines of a kitchen mixing bowl, or the slightly larger porcelain wash basin. The results had been disappointingly unspectacular. What was needed here was depth, you see, depth and the extra visual effects of blue water. Only then could I reproduce a scene anywhere approximating the dramatic one on the back of the cereal box. I bided my time. Barker kept watch, unless, of course, a Pond fly happened by.

A round galvanised tub, with soap-suds billowing over the

rim, was the centrepiece for both operations—the regular one, and the highly classified, top-secret one. An unpainted, wooden-framed wash-board with a ripply, translucent glass surface, protruded from the froth. In the uppermost portion was a recess suitable for accommodating a bar of Sunlight Soap. A box of Lux Soap Flakes stood nearby. There was also a sock containing a couple of cubes of "bluing." The sock was tied in a knot so the only way for the bluing to escape was for it to bleed through the fabric in which it was wrapped. Oddly, this blue chalky substance helped whiten whatever white items were being laundered, a concept about which I would have had my doubts had I not seen the miraculous results.

I'm sure Barker was puzzled at my fascination with the suds, the bluing, the wash-board, and the soap flakes. How could he know I was imagining the soft, slippery Lux Flakes to be snow? I sneaked a handful whenever Mom's back was turned. I wanted to sprinkle it from high above my head and watch it fall and disappear, like magic dust, into the washtub.

While he may not have understood my antics, he did seem to understand the 'sacredness' of laundry. He watched as, first, the mysterious brew was prepared in the tub. A pungent odour filled the air, evoking tears where there was neither sadness nor pain. Then, into that caustic sea of ammonia, bleach and bluing, softened only by a generous sprinkling of Lux, the sorted pile was ceremoniously immersed and allowed to soak. Next, each piece was plunged repeatedly into the foamy bath, and scrubbed against the 'altar' until purged of all filth and taint. After inspection and rinsing, the choice portions, still dripping, were draped upon a wire that stretched across the yard. When every piece had been pegged, a long stick was used, first to thrust the laden wire skyward like an offering to the sun, then as a prop to hold it there. A gentle breeze wafted through the cleansed offerings, and as they billowed, licked them dry.

Barker watched this strange ritual enacted weekly. He witnessed the seriousness with which Mom conducted it and he knew instinctively he should never dare to defile a human's laundry. I've seen some silly dogs in my time who liked to grab at laundry as it hung from the clothesline. They'd wrestle with it, tear it and drag it through the dirt, with not a clue they were committing some heinous offence. Yet this simple Pond Dog knew: "Don't ever touch the laundry."

Later, we got a brand new wringer/washer. What a thrill! Automation. No more bodybuilding exercises, since that's what wringing clothes by hand was. Just feed them sopping wet between the rollers, and watch them emerge, barely damp and

flatter than pancakes, on the other side.

This thing was fantastic. It had a timer, a drain hose, and even a gear-stick for adjusting the speed of the agitator. By the way, the gear-stick added a touch of realism when I pretended to be driving a race car with Barker as my co-driver. Another important feature: It had forward and reverse for the wringer part—quite handy for releasing mis-

chievous fingers or arms, depending on how quickly the would-be-rescuer could react.

I subsequently heard unconfirmed stories of at least two such incidents. In each case the victim's arm was allegedly trapped clean up to the armpit. The only solution was reverse gear—double indemnity.

Nevertheless, the feature I remember most vividly has nothing to do with its efficiency, or its mechanical genius. In fact, it may even seem frivolous. Yet, in some ways, it represents another important part in the tapestry of a Pond Dog's life.

There are certain sounds and smells that are just as much a part of that tapestry as are the visual depictions. Barker's world was made up of sights, sounds and smells. So to fully capture the flavour of this Pond Dog's life, you must know this about the washing machine, for I know Barker noticed it. I sure did.

That machine had rhythm. What with the agitator thumping, the water splashing, and the wet clothes slurping about, the beat was incredible—syncopated rhythms issuing from a washing machine. I would join in with the beat with my hands conga-drum style, and even danced a jig when the beat really started to get to me. That thing sure made laundry fun (though I'm not sure Mom felt that way. I never saw her dance over laundry). The only beat better than that had to belong to the Gombeys.

5

Music to a Pond Dog's ears

Since a dog's sense of hearing is so much keener than ours, Barker must have heard the merrymakers approaching long before we did. Surprisingly, as the sound drew nearer, passed by our house, rattled the windows, then faded into the distance, he never uttered a single sound of disapproval.

The music of the Gombeys never sounded sweeter than when the crowd wended its way down Pond Hill, along Pond Road, or around Curving Avenue. These impoverished communities, rich in culture, were always deserving of the best the Gombeys had to offer. And, no wonder! Many of the dancers and drummers came from these parts. So what better tribute to their families and friends than to stop by on those rare and special occasions to entertain them with a command performance?

Tradition dictated that each crowd of Gombeys follow its own route, but since Pond Road was a main thoroughfare, that stretch was almost unavoidable. From where we lived, we could hear Norford's Crowd start up in the distance. We'd know that in a short while they would be snaking their way down Pond Hill, turn right at the junction with Parson's Road, and soon

thereafter, be close enough for us to touch them—if we dared.

A hundred yards further left of that same junction is where Wilson's Crowd originated. They too, after a rousing opening salvo in their own yard, and a few brief courtesy calls on their immediate neighbours, would head our way. Even Merry Mice's Crowd eventually found its way past our house.

We knew automatically which group was which. They were so similar, yet so distinct. Each had its own beat, its own look, its own following, and its own character. Being non-partisan allowed us to enjoy the best that each had to offer. Furthermore, we got to do so from a ring-side seat. That's because "Shorty" Maynard lived right across the street from us. He played the bass drum for one of the crowds. The Warners lived in a little house next door to ours. The Gombey tradition ran thick in this family's blood, too (and still does). So we were guaranteed some spectacular performances right under our noses.

I can still remember the strange mixture of emotions the Gombeys evoked in me as a child of eight or nine. Foremost, there was fear. They seemed so tall to me. Indeed, many were close to six feet tall. Add to that height a three- or four-foot headpiece, and it becomes clear why they looked so imposing. But there was more. Their towering headdresses of peacock feathers whipped about in such frenzied commotion. Their painted masks depicted beady eyes, ruby lips and sardonic smiles, suggestive of an evil innocence. The captain's whistle summoned, scolded and commanded in sharp piercing shrieks. His menacing whip flailed about whenever he felt inclined to let it. Other dancers brandished brightly painted tomahawks, or bows and arrows with which to engage one another in exquisitely choreographed mock battle. Occasionally, one of them would toss his tomahawk high into the air, and catch it with such grace and ease, that he'd elicit gasps and cheers from the lively spectators.

As their procession meandered along, detouring into the little side roads and footpaths that led to the homes of certain 'privileged' clients, excitement and anticipation built. "The

Gombeys are coming!" someone would shout in gleeful response to the sound of approaching drums. Another dozen children scampered off to meet the dancing troupe. A few timid souls lingered paralysed with fear. Often these were ones who had been threatened and teased: "The Gombeys are going to get you!" Though never directed to me, I do recall hearing such ominous threats spoken by certain mean-spirited big brothers or big sisters, or even by some thoughtless but well-meaning parents. While I knew there was no such thing as the "boogie-man," the Gombeys were very real. It took me a few years before I was convinced they were harmless.

My fear was mixed with fascination, however. I'd shrink back, while wanting to draw closer, trembling at their feigned hostility, yet admiring their total lack of inhibition. They danced with such wild abandon, fuelled by the frenzied rhythms of the snare, kettle and bass drums. They were so light on their feet, it appeared at times that they hardly touched the ground. They leapt, and stomped, and swirled, and gyrated in complex dance patterns that every little boy in the neighbourhood seemed to have acquired at birth. Their fringed costumes, magnificent capes and splendid headgear exaggerated their every movement, adding to the excitement in the air. Meanwhile, the cacophonous sounds of the drums quickened the heartbeat, and tugged at the will, coaxing every bystander to join the fray, or at least, to follow it.

It was easy to get swept along in the flood of enthusiasm and merry-making and to forget the fear. Besides, I had Barker by my side.

"Come on, Barker. We'll just follow them to the next gate. We won't go out of view of the house."

I remember thinking: *I know we're not supposed to leave the yard without permission, but we won't go far. We'll be back so soon, Mom won't even miss us.* Of course, Barker was always game when it came to sneaking out of the yard. We set off in pursuit of the spirited crowd.

There are people who enjoy the Gombeys for a few minutes

and walk away satisfied. There are others who are entranced by them. They must follow them. They must dance with them. They must get inside those drums. They must chant and goad the dancers and drummers. They must completely immerse themselves in the experience, until either they are totally exhausted, or the drummers quit and go home. For them, it is sheer revelry.

Invariably, these are people from areas like Parson's Road, Curving Avenue, Friswell's Hill, Government Gate, Pond Hill, North Village, Happy Valley, Deep Dale, and Smith Hill. Not that they hold exclusive title to the Gombeys, mind you. Today, the Gombeys are a national treasure, a piece of folk art well preserved. It's just that if you could get some of those revellers to stand still long enough to ask them where they are from, the majority would cite one of the aforementioned places as their original home. I understand many parishes had Gombey troupes in the past, but where they have thrived is where their cultural roots have been strongest. Thus to this day there isn't a single Pond Dog who doesn't rally to the call of the Gombeys, or have to fight that urge to do so.

I believe every Pond Dog that ever lived, loved the sound of the Gombeys. How else could it be explained that, with all of the commotion they created, you never heard a dog barking at them? An old drunk would stagger along Parson's Road, singing hymns in raucous baritones, and every dog in the neighbourhood would go into a frenzy. A West Indian lady balancing bundles on her head, and offering home-made coconut cakes for sale, would call out, and the dogs would bark. A horse-drawn, buck-board-style wagon would come rattling down the road, and every dog, including Barker, would be livid. But the sweet, sweet racket of the Gombey drums was music to a Pond Dog's ears.

The truth is: No one from that area could resist their infectious rhythms. They had a way of reaching deep down inside you and triggering some genetic device already tuned to the same frequency. It made you want to move. It still does. I've seen adults, renowned in the community for their stolid reserve, abandon all composure under the influence of that irresistible beat. Old men and old women have become boys and girls again, and children have been lured miles away from home under the mesmerising spell of these pied pipers of Pembroke. Really, how could they ignore such a persuasive combination of brightly-coloured costumes, with fringed borders; black velvet capes decorated with ribbons, mirrors, beads and sequins; towering head dresses of iridescent peacock feathers; gauze-like face masks to conceal identities; electrifying acrobatics; uninhibited dancing; a swelling mob of chanting revellers; all to the accompaniment of that joyous, spirited drumming?

A brief glimpse of this travelling road show, as it passed by, never sufficed. There was instant addiction. The only way to get more was to follow. The decision to do so was impulsive—spontaneous. To this day I have contended that, if ever there was a litmus test by which to identify a true Pond Dog, it would be his reaction to the sounds of the Gombey drums.

Three hours and many miles later, Barker and I found ourselves in a strange neighbourhood. Nothing looked familiar. The Gombeys were taking a well-deserved break for refreshments in someone's house in Spanish Point. Barker was also taking a well-deserved break as he lay panting near my feet.

Oh, no! Where are we? What time is it? Boy, are we in trouble! How do we get home? Suddenly, my fear returned—not fear of the Gombeys—but of what awaited me when I arrived home, if I could ever find my way back.

"See what you made me do," I said to Barker (who else was there to blame?). "Why didn't you stop me? You'd better help us find our way home."

Barker sniffed the ground and began walking, then trotting. Soon we were racing along the North Shore, past Deep Bay, Berkeley Road, Ducking Stool, through Blackwatch Pass, right on course for home.

"How was Aunt Thel?"

Good. Mom thinks we've been at my cousin's house only yards away all this time. Barker and I had had such a great time. Why ruin it?

"Fine."

"That's funny. Aunt Thel said she saw you and Barker go prancing past her house hours ago following the Gombeys. Just wait 'til your father comes home, Mister."

Uh-oh, she said "Mister." That was serious. Only serious matters of discipline were referred to Dad. *Those Gombeys. This is all their fault.*

There was another sound that Barker acknowledged with barely a twitch of his ears. It was the mournful moan of the fishmonger's horn, announcing fresh fish for sale.

After a day's fishing, fishermen took to the streets to sell their catch. Using a flatbed pickup, an old Hillman, Morris Minor, or Ford Prefect car, or just a wheelbarrow lined with canvas, they cruised along Pond Road, each heralding his presence by blowing a conch shell fashioned into a horn. The resulting deep, mellow sound would echo throughout the neighbourhood, bringing people out of their homes and into the streets to buy fish—that is, if all of the criteria could be met.

First, it had to be the right kind of fish. Some people preferred jacks, and would buy them by the bunch. Others couldn't stand jacks:

"Too bony. Give me a good snapper any day."

Some sought mackerel. To others:

"Too strong! The house will smell like fish for a week!"

Others wanted a fish for baking. "Got any rockfish, or hamlets?"

Nothing else would do. After all, there'd always be another fish cart coming along...or another day.

Next came inspection. The fisherman always held up a specimen for the customer's approval. His expert hands could sense its weight. Hooking the hand-scale through the gills was just for confirmation, a mere formality. The potential buyer examined the fish with his or her own brand of expertise, visualising it in the frying pan or baking pan, no doubt. Then, if the mental picture was right: "How much?" Some dickering over the price, and a deal was struck.

Finally, the vendor threaded a strip of palmetto leaf up through the fish's gills and out of its mouth. He knotted both ends of the strand together to form a handle, and politely passed it to his valued patron, who gladly handed over a few shillings in exchange for a night's dinner. Another happy, satisfied customer.

I noticed that women usually bought smaller fish, just enough for supper that night. On the other hand, men seemed to take  great pride in walking away with the biggest fish available. Not that their reasons were entirely ego-related. You see, a big fish could yield several meals, including a hefty pot of chowder. A family could look forward to eating fish ad nauseam (so to speak). To this day, Dad takes great delight in buying a gargantuan fish and sharing it with the rest of the family.

"Got a nice-sized shark for me today?" someone would ask.

"Sure, lady. Saved this one just for you," he'd fib.

"Is it fresh?" she'd ask, hands on large hips, hanky with the money wrapped in it clutched in one fist.

"If it was any fresher it would bite you," he'd tease.

"What about the liver? Let's see the liver. Don't want no bad liver, you know…"

"Lady, look at this liver. It's healthier than mine!"

With that, another deal was sealed. Envious, covetous eyes would follow her as she walked away with her prize, all contemplating her tasty meal of shark hash, rice and sweet potatoes.

The aroma of cooked fish, be it fried, baked, boiled, grilled, or sautéed, would hang heavy in the still, damp air that evening, long after the echoes of the last conch shell blasts had faded.

But, alas, Barker could have none. If there was one thing we didn't feed him, it was fish bones. These were wrapped in thick newspaper and deposited in the trash-can for renegade cats to plunder at night. That wasn't the intent, mind you, but such was the effect, since the newspaper ploy seldom succeeded in concealing the strong scent of fish.

This gave rise to another familiar sound—one which did bring loud and incessant protests from Barker—the rattling of dislodged garbage pail lids by inconsiderate cats at three o'clock in the morning. Judging by their steady howls and hisses, apparently they found plenty in the papers worthy of comment.

Speaking of newspapers, there was one more sound that Barker knew well, and for which he reserved a special greeting. It was the welcome sound of Mr. Ford's motorised wheelchair. With a cheerfulness, determination and dedication unmatched, Mr. Ford would deliver the daily papers. I don't know how far afield his route stretched, but he sure carried a huge bundle of papers, enough for his regulars and anyone else who asked for a copy.

He was such a nice man—soft-spoken, polite, friendly, even to children, who according to the popular adult axiom of the day, were supposed to be seen but not heard. To see him huddled in his chair on those cold, damp mornings, blanket draped across his lap, canvas covering his precious cargo, money pouch hanging by a shoulder strap around his neck, filled me not with pity, but with admiration.

The chug, chug, chug of his motorcycle/wheelchair was an early-morning wake-up call. It was a symbol of continuity and predictability. It represented the 'village voice,' because it brought the daily news of the world to our threshold. The bark with which Barker greeted Mr. Ford, The Paper Man, was different, more like a friendly yelp of recognition. It was an expression of appreciation from all, including those of us still wrapped snugly in our warm beds. I used to wish for his safety on his lonely, arduous paper route, and that he'd sell every single newspaper he was carrying.

6

Quiet!
It's
Sunday!

The Pond and everything else was quiet on Sundays, particularly in the morning. It was a time when even the Pond Dogs retreated into repose. Barker certainly did. He did his best to guard the Sunday silence by refraining from needless barking. Mostly, he slept.

Children couldn't play outside lest they disturbed someone's legislated tranquillity. We'd be reprimanded for even whistling on a Sunday. "Hey, hey, hey! Cut that out!" It was sacrilege. So was playing rock and roll, jazz, calypso, or any other music but gospel. That was "inspirational music," I think they called it. No Gombey drumming on tins and boxes, no dancing, no running about the neighbourhood, no frivolity of any kind was allowed. Apparently, fun was outlawed, at least for the morning.

Everything and everyone had to be quiet. After all, people were worshipping or were supposed to be. They must have worshipped vicariously through the radio broadcasts, because those were the only sounds allowed to break the Sunday morning stillness. The air would be heavy with the sombre strains of a church organ and a choir singing maudlin hymns. Often our

neighbours joined in the choruses. They seemed to know all the words, yet strangely, they never left home to enjoy the real thing in person. I neither knew nor understood that many would be less than warmly welcomed; and that their very presence might cause offence to some. It had something to do with special seats curiously called 'rented' pews and the fact that unauthorised people who sat in them were made to move. There were murmurings about certain people not being accepted into certain churches. Such things were all too complex for an eight-year-old and a Pond Dog living in the 1950s to fathom. All we knew was that it contributed to the mood of Sunday mornings in the Pond.

"Does Barker know it's Sunday?" I asked my dad.

"Why do you ask that?"

45

"He hardly barks on Sundays, like he knows he's supposed to be quiet."

"I guess there's just not much to bark about."

"That doesn't stop him on other days."

I decided he could probably tell it was Sunday, if not by the sound of church music, then certainly by the familiar aroma of the traditional Bermuda Sunday breakfast. Codfish and potatoes, garnished with banana, hard-boiled egg, avocado, and optional tomato sauce, was a permanent fixture. He had to notice it. We did. What a welcome change from six days of Cream of Wheat or Corn Flakes.

Indeed, the whole idea about Sundays was: "Take a break from the day-to-day-routine." Many felt bound by religious tradition to pause and give thanks.

Not all of Sunday's quietude was imposed by religious tradition, however. Some of it was dictated by the irreligious revelries of the night before. How ironic that those of such irreverent behaviour should benefit from the reverence the community attached to Sundays.

Those who "stayed too long with the wine" on Saturday nights awoke with well-deserved hangovers. Yet there was undeserved solace in the serenity of Sunday mornings. The antidotes for their thudding headaches were silence—total, idle silence—and time.

First, though, they had to suffer the clanging rebuke of the neighbouring church bells. Then, to the inescapable drone of an Anglican clergyman's ecclesiastical chants, or the slightly more animated tones of an A.M.E. pastor granted equal broadcast time, they could await full sobriety.

Meanwhile, they vowed never to repeat the sins and follies of the night before. We all knew how quickly such promises would be forgotten.

We used to watch, with perplexity, drunken men both young and old, or maybe they were just young men who seemed old. They'd stagger and weave their way along Pond Road, riding the undulating road like a surfboard novice. Maybe Barker perceived something menacing in their unsteady gait and their incoherent mutterings. He definitely barked some of his harshest reprimands as they stumbled past our house. Invariably, that would be in the wee hours of Sunday morning. By daybreak they'd be in a heap somewhere along the roadside sleeping it off. At best, they slept oblivious to the ridicule and disdain of passersby. At worst, they awoke to find themselves the victims of self-inflicted violence. The bumps and bruises they discovered when sober mystified them.

If there was pleasure in dizziness, vomitting and collapsing, I asked myself, why were people so miserable when they were sick? If there was so much joy in celebrating to the point of drunkenness, why didn't these men look like they were having fun? Thus, even in those spartan surroundings, I learned a valuable lifelong lesson: Merriment of this kind comes with a price—payment of which, when due, is mercilessly demanded.

The mellow tones of Sundays continued through lunchtime when families sat down to eat. That's right. Whole families sat around a common, set table. In fact, boys and girls had to learn how to set a table correctly. It was one of a number of unisex chores that were mandatory. We just thought they were decreed from on high, so we did them without complaint. Complaining wasn't allowed either—not on Sundays, not ever.

Sometimes the venue for Sunday lunch was Grandma's house. For us, this meant a walk up the hill via a shortcut—a bumpy dirt path that brought us onto Curving Avenue. Then we'd cut through the Stevens' yard and arrive at Grandma's doorstep famished. That's because the route was seasoned with such delightful roasted smells that emanated from every humble dwelling along the way. It was an act of kindness not to take Barker through that gauntlet. Besides, what better time was there for him to make one of his famous escapes to the Pond than on a lazy, quiet Sunday?

The old wooden homestead was cozy and welcoming. The kitchen had mostly homemade furnishings. I often wondered if Dad made any of the benches when he was young. For some reason, perhaps it was fashionable at the time, kitchen table-cloths were always checkered. There was no garish lighting, just daylight and a single bulb which couldn't have been more than thirty watts. It dangled from the low ceiling by a braided cord. The well-worn linoleum was proof this was the busiest room in the house. Grandpa ate in the kitchen like hired help. I wondered why he never joined us, but dared not ask. We had to be quiet, speaking only when spoken to. Not having had much practice, though, we were always somewhat shy when someone did speak to us, or when finally asked a question.

"Don't be bashful," they'd say. "Speak up."

What if we did? I later wondered. What if, on one of those occasions, we really did speak up? What if we started talking, then went on, and on, and on, expressing our opinions about everything under the sun? Wouldn't they have been shocked?

After lunch we had to hang around. After all, this was a visit, not a fuel stop. The grown-ups talked. One of my aunts usually opened the blinds in the front room on Sundays and allowed us to sit in there amid the fern stands and knick-knacks. We'd gaze around in fascination at ancient pictures of Grandma and Grandpa, my dad and his brothers and sisters, and other unrecognisable kinfolk.

Although everything looked so old and interesting, we didn't dare handle a single relic. It was "See, but don't touch," a rule we fully understood.

Later, on the occasional Sunday afternoon, Dad would take me to a football game at the Sports Arena. We called it The Box. It was the home field of the Key West Rangers who later became the P.H.C. Zebras. With a blast of the referee's starting whistle, the day returned from its state of suspended animation. It totally erased from memory the earlier silence.

I still remember watching games between such teams as the West End Rovers, Pembroke Juniors, Key West Rangers and Dock Hill Rangers, and being enthralled by the whole experience. The Box erupted with cheers and shouts as the two elevens took to the field. The noisy, electrifying atmosphere was the antithesis of Sunday mornings.

Before long, I was identifying players by their pet names. There was Bummy, Townsey, Froggy, and Junior; Charlie, Scorchy, Liney and Turp; Cheesey, Flat-top, Pop and Dewey, to name a few. They all played their hearts out for us, but I noticed how fickle the fans were. One minute they cheered their heroes, the next, they scolded them mercilessly.

How unfair, I thought. I wanted to cheer for everybody, on both teams.

Dad gave me pocket money to buy roasted peanuts and a bottle of mineral, and if we hadn't just come from Grandma's, a hot-dog with mayonnaise and pickle.

In the meantime, Barker was far from my thoughts. I was too busy enjoying myself. Besides, he'd be home when I got there, or shortly thereafter if he'd opted to escape for the day. I'd feed him something repulsive, or, maybe we'd be finished with the bone of that leg of lamb. Whatever. He understood. Pond Dogs are good that way—so undemanding.

7

Little things that amused

*L*ittle things amuse little minds, or so the saying goes. It's a criticism of those whose minds are preoccupied with trivial, inconsequential things, but I now consider the statement to be highly complimentary. The ability to take 'little things' and with a fertile imagination find amusement in them, is a gift.

The little mind that's amused by little things won't be easily bored. To me, that's a large, limitless mind. The mind that's amused only by big things is the one that's limited, because it's wholly dependent upon the sensational, the graphic, the spectacular, for stimulation.

For Barker and me there was none of the latter. Instead, we indulged in gruelling contests of tug-o'-war. I often let him win just for the joy of seeing him scamper off with his prey and shake it violently until it was dead. That rag or rope didn't stand a chance.

Sometimes, I ran back and forth, trailing the bait tantalisingly close to his nose, daring him to grab it. He always accepted the challenge. It allowed him to pretend he was a wild animal. Whether this was all for his own amusement or mine, I never knew. Nevertheless, he attacked repeatedly and, with such fervor, I couldn't imagine he was simply humouring me. We tussled, tugged and taunted, until only a mutually declared truce saved us from total exhaustion. For variation, I sometimes substituted a ball, a stick, or an old shoe, all to equal effect. Barker loved it.

At least I was including him in the action, unlike the times when we children were confined to the indoors. Any number of offences could warrant such draconian sentencing: Measles, mumps, whooping cough, chicken-pox, colds, ringworm, rainy days. At other times, it was just because our parents said so.

"You're not to go outside. Do you understand?"

"Yes, Momma. Yes, Deddy" (It was probably some test of obedience).

We thought it so arbitrary at the time. "Stay inside" seemed to be a cure for everything. We'd simply have to make the best of such periods of unwarranted persecution. With Mom and Dad a safe distance away at work, the 'suffering' could begin.

Barker, tormented by the sounds of gaiety that leaked through stone walls and shuttered windows, could only respond half-heartedly to our laughter and childish squeals. At those times, we were so thoughtless, so inconsiderate of his feelings, so oblivious to his existence.

How he must have longed to see what we were doing that caused us such delight. How he must have wished he could be a part of it. How he must have hoped we'd one day break the rule and smuggle him inside. There he could have seen, first hand, the havoc we wreaked, as we transformed our beds into trampolines and tried to touch the ceiling. He could have shared our euphoria as we broke each other's record for the longest-lasting-headstand-executed-on-the-bed-with-feet-propped-against-the-wall. He could have joined in the riotous laughter our pillow fights evoked, or witnessed our skillful manoeuvres as we ran and slid in stockinged feet on floors made slippery with talcum powder. He could have known the reason for those plaintive cries, which temporarily silenced our merriment, when one of us crashed into the furniture, or worse, a wall.

Poor Barker could see none of this. He could try only to imagine the source of such sounds of bedlam and add his voice in support. What he did seem to know was, in our parents' absence, we were doing things forbidden. We would need a signal as a warning of their return. Here is where he became our accomplice in mischief.

Before Mom or Dad even set foot in the yard, Barker barked so frantically we'd be fools not to know it was time to be sick again. There'd be a mad scramble as we inspected the house, and tried to set things back in order. Then, there was just enough time for us to adopt a demeanour befitting the reason for our confinement. Thanks to him, they'd enter to find us as tranquil and innocent as they'd left us, the suspicious fragrance of talcum in the air notwithstanding.

Once, while chasing a loose ball that had run amok in the living room, we knocked over the knick-knack stand, breaking a couple of precious, delicate ornaments. We were on our own that day. Barker couldn't help us, neither could our skillfully contrived explanation.

You see, this truck came rumbling past. It created such a tremor, the whole house shook. You could even hear the windows rattle. We thought that whole, rickety knick-knack stand was going to collapse. Honest. The next thing we knew, two figurines were lying on the floor in pieces. Yes. Of course. What a plausible explanation.

Well, at least I thought so. Why was it so hard for my folks to swallow? What gave parents the ability to see right through us, and know when we were lying? I'd rehearsed that explanation in my mind repeatedly. It sure seemed to me to have a ring of truth. What went wrong?

Barker heard a different sound issuing from the house that night. It wasn't the sound of laughter.

Back then, parents punctuated their disciplinary lectures with the 'licks' they dished out. Each word was worth one lick. For example:

"Didn't I tell you not to play in the house?"

Ordinarily, that's ten words (Maybe three 'punctuation' marks). But that was too short when you deserved "a good flogging." So, they stretched it out.

"Didn't I tell – tell – tell – tell – tell you not – not – not to play – play – play in the house – house – house – house – house? Didn't I? Didn't I? Didn't I?" See! Twenty-eight words…and the possibility of at least twenty punctuations. Some parents punctuated every word.

Later, while you were still smarting from the discipline, they explained that this was not about breaking the figurines. It was about failing to be truthful.

You mean, if I'd greeted you at the door with the broken knick-knacks in hand and confessed: "Hi, Mom! Hi, Dad! By the way, I broke these while playing ball in the house," I wouldn't have been punished? Somehow, I found that hard to believe.

On rainy days, we'd press our forlorn faces against the window panes and watch the water in the lower backyard approach flood stage. We'd watch the patterns the pelting rain created on the surface of that rising tide. How we longed to be outside! We wanted to feel the rain sting our faces. We yearned to jump and splash around in that private puddle growing before our eyes, but the orders were strict and explicit: "Stay inside!"

We envied Barker. *He* got to stay out in the rain whenever *he* wanted. Sometimes he just curled up in a ball, in what must be the foetal position for dogs, and let the rain beat down on him. When he'd had enough, he crawled into his house soaked and satisfied. *He* never got sick or caught a cold because of being out in the rain.

Why did *we* have to be confined so? Didn't we have rainboots? What was the point of having rainboots if we couldn't test them out in the rain? When would we get to wear them? On a dry, sunny day? I'd tried that. My feet got very hot, and

sweated a lot. Yes, we did wear them to school on rainy days, but that didn't count.

Wait a minute! If we were allowed (even expected) to go out in the rain to get to school, why couldn't we go out and play in it on non-school days? And, did this mean if I 'accidentally' dropped something out of the window, because I was opening the window to get some air, I couldn't dash out there to get it? Or did it mean that we couldn't open the kitchen door and launch a few homemade sailboats? What if one should sink, or get stuck hard and fast against the wall? What if all of them did? Could I not hurry out there and retrieve them? Well, what if, after dashing out there, on this urgent mission of mercy, I accidentally splashed more water on myself than I'd intended? Would it be all right to linger out there a little longer, since I was already wet, anyhow?

Clearly, this brilliant young lad was destined to become a lawyer. I could convince myself that it was perfectly acceptable —even necessary—to disregard the Stay Inside Rule.

The problem was I couldn't persuade the judge, jury and executioner to spare me the consequences of my disobedience. Naturally, my sisters decided to turn state's evidence as soon as Mom or Dad set foot in the door. Their expert, eyewitness testimony, corroborated by strong, circumstantial evidence (damp clothes, soggy underwear, my sneezing), would easily establish my guilt. Of course, none of my aforementioned arguments worked. So I had to implicate the witnesses ("Their boats got stuck, and I had to run outside to get them. Besides, while I was running outside, they were reaching out trying to catch the raindrops!"). After all, misery does love company.

That's what I liked about Barker. He may have been nothing but a Pond Dog, but he never told on you. I considered him to be more loyal than my sisters. Well, at least more sympathetic. He knew about siblings and their vyings for approval, recognition and attention. He understood my need for respite from the constant compromises imposed upon a boy with two sisters. He witnessed a little boy's oafishness pitted against the co-ordination, daintiness and finesse of two girls playing jacks, skipping rope, or playing hopscotch. He saw me gamely trying to enjoy myself, though my turns were always so long in coming, yet so quickly over. So he knew I couldn't help rebelling a little from time to time. That's when he'd be there for me, and we'd play tug-o'-war and other 'guy' stuff.

Such were the 'little things' that amused us. We were content to chase butterflies, bees, crickets, or grasshoppers, and hold them captive in a ventilated mayonnaise bottle for observation. We were thrilled to track the piercing buzz of a singer to its source on a hot, lazy, summer afternoon. That was an art.

Singers were plentiful then. Correctly known as cicadas, their shrill songs used to resonate through the summer air, particularly in open spaces. They made a most unique sound by vibrating the abdominal sections of their bodies vigourously. Old cedar trees were the most favoured haunts of these giant flying insects. From there, their thick bodies and diaphanous wings perfectly  camouflaged, they could sing to their hearts' content.

Their sounds provided constant background noise for the summer days. Occasionally, one flew closer than usual. We knew that because the sound it made was no longer a distant background noise. It became deafening, dominating, distinct.

"A singer! Let's go, Barker!" Off we'd dash in chase of the elusive singer, I with jar in hand, Barker puzzled about what we were chasing but enjoying the excuse to run, nonetheless. Sometimes, several other children joined the chase.

"He's over here."

"Sh-h-h! You'll scur 'im."

"Grab him!"

"What, with my bur hands?"

"Bie, grab de thing. He won' bite you."

"You grab him."

"See dat! You let him get away."

Of course, if Barker happened to be on the scene, the singer's chances of escaping were even better. This dog wasn't exactly the master of good timing when it came to barking excitedly. Or was he?

What simple fun it was to hold a jar to your ear and listen to the symphony of your very own collection of honey bees. What a rush of adrenaline we experienced from snaring lizards by the neck with artfully contrived nooses made of grass—a practice which never struck me as particularly cruel until my father said: "How would you like for someone to do that to you?" and made me release my victim.

I wondered why the lizards didn't struggle or protest more if they didn't like it. Why did they just sit there with those stupid smiles on their faces and let us slip the nooses over their heads? Nevertheless, after that rebuke from my dad, I developed a conscience that would not allow me to enjoy that pastime ever again. I renounced lizard-catching, and became something of a neighbourhood animal rights activist.

"How'd you like it if someone did that to you?" I parroted, whenever I encountered other children doing the very thing for which I'd once been scolded. For the most part, my protests fell on deaf ears.

No wonder. I was among youths who took delight in lizard fights, stoning frogs, slaying birds with slingshots, and splitting tops in half! That's how mean they were. Mind you, they didn't intend to be mean. They were just Pond Dogs having fun. If a shiny, brand new top was automatic prey, what chance did a lowly frog, or lizard, or bird stand?

Boys bought toy spinning tops for a shilling and immediately set about converting them. This involved the removal of the benign, half-inch tip and replacing it with a lethal, three- or four-inch nail, filed to a point. Thus armed, the assassins then stalked the neighbourhood or school yard in search of victims— other tops.

"Let's play 'pickins.'"

"O.K." Someone would mark an X on the ground to start the action. "Furthest from the centre goes down."

Zing, zing, zing. The brightly-coloured tops would fly as each player took aim at the target. The string used for spinning the top was also used to measure whose nail mark was furthest from centre. The one whose top was judged to have missed by the greatest margin paid the penalty.

"Aw right, put that nice, fat, juicy top down. I wanna get a bite of it." That top now became the target.

"Das right, X marks de spot."

"Watch me ring down on it." With a whipping action, one boy released his missile from its coiled string with all the force he could muster. Invariably, he struck his target with pinpoint accuracy. The ultimate object was to completely destroy the target. However, to earn another turn, he had to either hit the target or deliver his top, still spinning, to the spot and make sure it at least touched the target. Failure meant having to surrender his own top to replace the target top.

"That was just an inky. Watch this." Another flailing arm and zinging top. A chip of wood from the victim went flying.

"Oooh! A chip."

Sometimes, there was a feeding frenzy, as open season was declared on some hapless victim. Arms flailed wildly, as missile after deadly missile inflicted damage. An "inky" (a mere puncture in the target) was not enough. That was just drawing first blood. The marauders gathered around to inspect the tips of their warheads for forensic evidence theirs was the one that inflicted the wound. Then they swarmed in for the kill with another flurry of flailing arms and whirring tops. Wicked, merciless laughter celebrated the damage.

"Split it! Split it open!" There was no respite until the target lay split asunder, and the owner was reduced to a pool of tears.

"Bie, look what you done to my top." A split top earned the executioner a notch on his weapon, as well as the undying admiration of his peers.

I suppose the top manufacturers thought they were producing an innocuous little toy. Their vision was of innocent little children amusing themselves while trying to get these things spinning, and giggling with delight over their modest successes. Right! Little did they know bands of young psychopaths were modifying their product for such sinister purposes.

That's why I kept my prized New York (red and blue) top stashed securely at home. There I could share it privately with Barker in the safety of our own back yard. No one was going to play 'pickins' with my treasured top. It was a gift from our neighbour, who worked on board the *Queen of Bermuda*. Besides, I wasn't very good at 'playin' pickins.' Whenever I tried to practise at home, Barker would sit on the X mark or snatch the target top and run. When top season rolled around, I made sure I carried a cheaper, dispensable top. Just in case.

8
Something old, something new

You could give Barker an old shoe or a brand new rubber ball, and he would be equally satisfied. Likewise, we learned to make the best of the old things until something new came along.

For example, someone would be saving for a new bike. That could take what seemed like forever to a child, particularly if their principal means of income was cashing in empty mineral bottles. Waiting until their parents could afford to buy them a bike could take almost as long. On the other hand, they could find an old bike frame, attach a couple of wheels, and be mobile within hours.

"All we need is a front wheel. Dis one's bent."

"What about a seat?"

"Plus its only got one pedal an' no brakes."

"We don' need all dat. One o' you can sit on de crossbar, one can sit on de handlebars, an' I can stan' up. Den we can range off de heel."

"You sure?"

"Yah, bie. Um done it plenty o' times."

"But how we go'n stop?"

"Dat's easy! De guy on de handlebars can jus press his feet 'gainst de wheel."

"S'pose we steel can't stop?"

"Well…we jus' jump off, dassall. If de bike gets mashed up, we can always go out de puhwn an' get another frame."

"My deddy said his gon' buy me a new bike wif front and back brakes, an' a headlight, an' a dual seat, an' mud-flaps and errything."

"Bie, ya deddy eeng buyin' you no bike."

"Yes he is!"

"Oh yah? When? Mus' be in de yur 2000, i'n it?"

"You wait, an' when I get it, you eeng goin' ride it either."

Another time when new things abounded was on the first day back to school. "All school children shall wear uniforms to school," our forefathers had declared. So after a summer of codeless dress and going barefooted, it was always, to me, such an oddity to see scores of us identically and neatly dressed and groomed.

Everyone was so transformed. Boys had haircuts. Brown shoes were spit polished. If not, they were squeaky new because unrestrained feet had grown a size or two. Our new khaki shorts sported razor-sharp creases. The girls wore navy blue gimps. Crisp, blinding white shirts with stiff, starched collars, a school tie, and navy blue socks that stayed up because there was life in their elastic tops, completed the miraculous transformation.

Barker probably knew something was in the air days before the 'big day.' Whenever we had something new, he was relegated to second fiddle, and for back-to-school we wallowed in new things: A brand, spanking new book-bag with all new stuff inside. A new pencil box with new pencils, new ruler, new eraser, new fountain pen (ball-points were not allowed), new crayons, and new blue exercise books with the Queen's face on the cover and some useful tables on the back (just in case, while gallivanting all summer, we'd forgotten everything we'd ever learned). A new lunch kit and thermos (or, among the genuinely underprivileged, new brown bag and mayonnaise bottle, with waxed paper seal under the screw-on top).

Barker yielded to our preoccupations without protest. I think he knew that newness was fleeting, and that after a few days, weeks at most, pencils would be snapped in two and riddled with teeth marks. Rulers would lose their straight edges. Crayons would be reduced to stubs. Exercise books would be full of inkblots, dog-ears, and red-inked correction marks. Book bags would be scuffed. Hopalong Cassidy lunch kits would be dented, and Batman and Robin thermoses would be transformed into rattles. He didn't mind waiting until the novelty wore off and something new became something old.

In the meantime, there was the amusing diversion of watching familiar neighbourhood ruffians and riff-raff parade by, all decked out in regulation attire, in strict adherence to Central School's inviolable code.

Few things drew more attention than a new haircut. According to convention, 'privileged' boys got regular haircuts—not good haircuts, necessarily, just regular. Some, preferring not to be so 'privileged,' totally ignored convention. And who could blame them? They'd seen some of the bad haircuts, the crude results of somebody's attempts at barbering.

Often, it was a parent who fancied himself to be a competent barber. At times, it was a neighbourhood barber who fancied himself competent. I considered it robbery that anyone should charge money for butchering little boys' heads like that. We won't even speak of those who played barber by experimenting on willing, and not-so-willing subjects.

In our house, it was Dad who cut my hair. Ironically, he paid an expert to cut his, yet when it came to mine, he felt compelled to break out his do-it-yourself kit. Thankfully, he was pretty good at it. His hand-powered clippers did pinch my scalp, and tug at a few hairs at times, but I dared not flinch too much. Each jerk of the head meant another patch of hair accidentally removed. So I learned to grin and bear Dad's little slips. At least when I ventured outside, I could walk tall. Sure, there were a few snide remarks, but not cruel, merciless ridicule. That was reserved for the exceptionally bad cases.

Certain boys were cursed. They regularly appeared in public with haircuts that were bound to make them laughing-stocks. Obviously, their shearers gave no thought to styling, head shape, self-esteem, or aesthetics. Their aim was simply to remove the excess hair in the quickest way possible. What weapons they used to inflict such devastation remains a mystery. But the results were unmistakably humiliating.

It was enough to force a boy to wear his cap way down over his naked ears, but that would only arouse more suspicion about what he was hiding. He could  try to stay out of sight until his hair grew back, but that too, was impractical. By the time he resurfaced, it would be time for another bad hair-cut. He'd never see the light of day. He could opt to fight for his honour, but what honour was there in looking like that? No. His best option was to bravely face the music and take whatever teasing was dished out. The more he reacted, the worse the teasing became. Better he learn to take it, and laugh at himself.

Dogs have a way of pricking up their ears and cocking their heads in a quizzical gesture that says, "What's this?" or "What happened to you?" I saw that reaction from Barker many times. Perhaps it was his way of expressing sympathy. Then again, maybe he was laughing, too.

He gave me that same puzzled look whenever he saw me all dressed up. Was it that he didn't recognise me at first? Or did I look odd to him? Did he feel left out, because we were going somewhere he wasn't invited? Or, was it feelings of betrayal that registered on his face? Had not he and I romped barefooted in the yard only hours before? Why was I now not even willing to come near him? So what if I had a fancy new suit and brand new, blue suede shoes? Was that any reason to ignore him?

Still, he barked excitedly as we lined up to have our pictures taken—without him. He watched longingly as we primped, preened, and posed for the camera. Then, forgiving us for our preoccupation, he gave us the usual warm and frantic sendoff. Pond Dogs are like that. They're used to being ignored, but they never hold it against you.

The neighbourhood was abuzz late one afternoon. We were playing alleys in the Thompsons' yard, two houses up the hill from ours, when we got the news.

"The Smiths just got a TV!"

"A *what*?"

"*T–V*. It stands for television. It's like a radio, but you can see people on a screen talking and doing things. They show movies and cartoons, too."

"Oh yah. I think I saw one o' doze in Masters' windah dahn tahn."

The Smith family who lived across from the Thompsons were the first ones in the neighbourhood to get a TV. At six o'clock that evening, everybody flocked to their porch to see the mysterious, blue-grey, illuminated picture on their brand new console. In true neighbourly fashion, they obligingly opened their windows and turned the set toward the porch for all to share. Forty eyes must have peered through the porch windows that evening at snowy outlines on the rounded screen.

"I see something!" a voice in the gallery exclaimed.

"Looks like a cowboy on a white horse," added another.

"We only have rabbit's ears now," said Mr. Smith somewhat apologetically. "The picture will be much clearer when we get an outside antenna."

For a while, the only programming available was from Kindley Air Force Base. Later, ZBM signed on from their tiny

studio in Hamilton. TV fare was limited mainly to evenings. During the day, we watched test patterns.

Barker couldn't understand what all the excitement was about. He'd rather take an excursion to his favourite playground where the action was live. TV was only sight and sound. In The Pond he could indulge all five senses and get exercise at the same time. He could roam the wide open spaces, roll in the dew-drenched grass or gallop across the sandy desert. He could rifle through the garbage, wrestle with an over-sized pond rat or chase a hovering dragonfly. His was interactive entertainment at its best, for which TV was no match.

It would take decades before we would reach the point where densely populated neighbourhoods would take on the appearance of ghost towns, their yards and playgrounds devoid of childish laughter and play. In those days TV was a novelty, a stranger yet to truly make its presence felt.

Most children still preferred the outdoors. Indeed, confining us to indoors was the equivalent of tying Barker to that stake in the yard. We relished being outside, the longer, the better. Our hearts sank whenever we heard our names being called to summon us inside.

"Can't we play a little longer? It's not dark yet," we pleaded, as shadows lengthened then disappeared into twilight. We'd play frantically, as if trying to wring out every drop of available time as the evening darkness and the hordes of hungry mosquitoes descended upon us.

Something as old and commonplace as playing outside never lost its appeal. Perhaps today's 'hanging out' is not so new after all.

9

Pirates and oleanders

The oleanders which skirted the ditch were thick and tall, their sinewy boughs so supple and strong. On any given day they could be instantly transformed according to our childhood whims.

For example, a choice branch might be the sturdy back of a bucking bronco. With scarcely a stretch of the imagination, one of us could sit astride our mount with the confidence of a rodeo cowboy and hold on for dear life as a playmate released the wild horse from its corral. We figured out a way to simulate this by rocking and swaying the tree bough violently. The horse tired only when the partner did, at which point rider and partner switched roles and the fun resumed anew. Many a wild stallion was tamed out there in The Pond amid the oleanders.

Yet, having drunk our fill of bronco-busting, we were not about to become idle or bored. In an instant, we could be transferred to the deck of a sailing ship on a storm-tossed sea. This time, we stood on the very same boughs, clutching the tangled rigging above as our 'ship' ploughed its way through treacherous waters. We were pirates, and our ship was in danger of sinking, taking with it all of our treasure and the spoils of our conquests. It took every ounce of our strength and skill to keep the ol' tub afloat.

The ditch beneath us added a nice touch of realism, and in retrospect, an element of danger. That's because the more adventurous and daring (translated: Disobedient and foolhardy) climbed aboard a crate and actually paddled about in the ditch, à la Tom Sawyer and Huckleberry Finn. The rest of us could only stand agape at such pluck. Such blatant rebellion. Such folly. Somehow, their acts of disobedience seemed worse than ours.

Really, either way, there was bound to be retribution. The orders had been explicit: "Stay out of The Pond." "Do not play around The Pond." Either of the foregoing incidents violated that edict. It mattered not that we tried to rationalise that in the former instance we were never really *in* The Pond, just kind of hovering *over* it. Or that we were playing in the field bordering The Pond and accidentally wandered a bit too close, maybe while looking for a lost ball, or something. This was not about semantics. It was about disobedience, and about how one of us could have drowned.

Just as we always knew when Barker had transgressed, someone always knew when we had. What's more, parents had a way of homing in on the issue with such precision. Their penetrating interrogations really tested your character, forcing either an admission of guilt, or an outright lie. Most of us knew, or else we learned the hard way, that it was better to admit guilt than to be caught in a lie. And, sooner or later, you *were* caught.

I have a theory. Parents must have had some kind of intelligence network in those days. They probably made deals with one another to spy on us and take notes. When we sneaked off somewhere, safe in the knowledge that no one would know, neighbourhood spies recorded our every move. They scanned the neighbourhood with special radar surveillance equipment, and tracked these little blips wherever they went. Then these secret agents reported the movements of the blips to Command Central.

They were very good at their covert activities too, because they never blew their covers. And, judging from the outcries that could be heard later, I suspect that many a blip was identified, apprehended and punished, not a few with an oleander switch—the instrument of choice for certain extremist disciplinarians in the region of The Pond.

Oh, the versatility of the oleander! A rod of discipline one moment, a perennial bouquet the next. It decorated our landscape in a riot of colour, sweetening the air with its heavenly fragrance, yet it was possessed of other more fiendish and seldomlauded properties.

For example, the younger, more slender branches could be stripped of their leaves and bent into a very efficient bow. A length of builder's twine was a must for stringing the bow.

Where, though, was a lad to find a rare commodity like builder's twine? There was only one likely place.

I happened to know about the limitless supply in Dad's dresser draw. Surely it was there for the taking. Why else would a full-grown man be hoarding all of that string? He obviously intended that I should use it, discreetly, of course. So I raided Dad's bureau drawer whenever I needed a bit of heavy twine, two feet here for my top; three or four feet there for a bow. Naturally, my playmates needed some, too. Make that ten feet here, twelve feet there. When Dad finally noticed that his supply of twine was dwindling, I must say, he took it rather well.

"That's funny," he said, "I thought I had more line than this."

"Me, too!" I replied, wondering why I had the strange feeling he knew all along what I had been doing.

Pond sticks made excellent arrows, bottle caps, the perfect arrow-heads. Now that I think of it, what we had there was a lethal weapon. Oh-h-h-h! So that's why our parents forbade them. That's why they went on about poking someone's eye out, and things like that. And we thought they were just trying to be mean. Word had it parents simply didn't want their children to have any fun. Hence, all the restrictive rules.

"Don't throw stones." How could a boy have any fun in life if he couldn't throw stones? It was exercise. A test of strength, co-ordination, masculinity. How else would he know how good his aim was, or how far he could throw a stone? And the reasons for this stifling edict? "You might knock someone's eye out." "Stones don't have eyes," we were constantly reminded.

"No fighting with sticks." See? Another one! Just when we were about to get into one of those epic, mock sword fights between Zorro and the bad guys, or Ivanhoe and the knights of evil; just when Robin Hood and his Merry Men were poised to confront The Sheriff of Nottingham and his men, or two rival bands of swashbuckling pirates were about to duel it out over the issue of who shall rule the waves, they took our swords! We were hamstrung without swords, not to mention severely limited as to our choices of games to play. And the reason given for this injunction? "You might poke someone's eye out."

"No slingshots." There went another innovative product of the oleander. The best slingshots were fashioned from the perfect Y-shaped boughs of the young plants. A strip of rubber from an inner-tube, or better yet, two strips with a piece of sneaker tongue properly attached, and voila! Lethal Weapon Number 4. Pride of India berries were the ammunition of choice, with small pebbles a close second (or as back-up ammo). Only the most criminally-minded dared to consider using truly deadly projectiles, namely, staples, marbles or ball-bearings. But lest we be tempted to experiment, slingshots were outlawed. That was definitely good news for lizards, birds, and any moving thing that represented a potential target. Besides, "you could knock somebody's eye out with one of those things."

Of course, our parents were absolutely right about all of the above. Their sanity and respect for the sanctity of sight undoubtedly saved many an eye. We would just have to "beat our swords into ploughshares" and "learn war no more" just like Isaiah says in the Bible.

That wasn't easy for some who were accustomed to life 'round The Pond. After all, who didn't secretly want to be Robin Hood, Tarzan, the Phantom, or a Musketeer, a cowboy, an Indian, or a pirate? So like Barker, we too occasionally succumbed to the call of The Pond, and armed with our contraband weapons, sneaked off for the occasional frolic among the oleanders and tall grass.

Other kids were born naturals. They didn't have to sneak out there. They roamed wherever they pleased, or so it seemed. During the summer holidays, and even on certain school days, they virtually lived in The Pond. It was (I'm told) the perfect place for playing hooky too. (Truancy is the preferred word here, but hooky seems much more appropriate. It's a more earthy term, better suited to The Pond. Truancy was for kids of less humble status. The rest played hooky.)

I think once in a while Barker simply played hooky and hung around The Pond, the best hooky ground there was. In some ways, we both had the same problem, so I knew exactly how he felt. The Pond was forbidden, yet it had so much to offer—too much to ignore, or resist. Opportunity and adventure lay a-begging. Only by special parental indulgence could we ever hope to roam there, free of guilt and fear of being found out. No parent was ever going to consent to that. What else was a Pond Dog to do? There was no choice but to sneak out there now and then. It was like having an amusement park in your back yard, but being forbidden to set foot in it. Sooner or later, the lure of the rides and games was bound to get to you.

10

Bargains galore!

The Pond had this alluring quality back then, in the late 1950s and 1960s, not just for Barker but for boys in the area, too. Perhaps this was due in part to the fact that it was 'forbidden territory' for some of us, but also because of the bargains it offered. Whether you went there in search of something specific, or just to browse, you seldom left empty-handed. The place was a veritable treasure-trove, a gold mine. It was the crude forerunner of the modern-day shopping mall. Best of all, everything was free. Later, this open-air market would become the source of materials for every major construction project. So that at any given time throughout the neighbourhood, kids could be found building clubhouses, forts, flat-bottomed punts, dog houses, even rabbit hutches and chicken coops.

Who would have thought of actually purchasing lumber to build a shed, a cart, or a doghouse? Unthinkable! Lovely crates were piling up over there, waiting to be burned. Wasn't it far better to dismantle and recycle them, nails and all?

What fine, smooth, shiny nails they were. I used to think they were wonderful, so unlike our nails. Ours were blunt, and unat-

tractive. Years later, I was to learn why the shiny nails rusted so quickly and the dull ones didn't. I was to learn about the chemistry of rusting and galvanisation, and how the latter protects against the former. Couched in there was a greater lesson about looking beyond the shiny exterior. It was a lesson about quality and how to recognise it.

Who in his right mind would actually go out and buy a part for his bicycle? Indeed, who would buy a bicycle? We all knew that they—and their parts—came from The Pond. Cotter pins, tyres, axles, handlebars, reflectors, wheel rims, spokes, inner-tubes, pedals, brake shoes, bearings, chains, sprockets, fenders, nuts, bolts, frames, whole bikes—whatever you needed was there for the taking. Our neighbourhood was filled with not only mongrel dogs, but with an equal number of mongrel bikes as well.

A wooden box from The Pond was a treasure for any boy fortunate enough to get his hands on one. An old baby-carriage with wheels intact was another. Finding both during the same visit truly made sneaking out there worthwhile:

"Hey, you lot. Look what I found—baby-carriage wheels."

"I saw um first!"

"No, you di'nt."

"Yes, I did."

"But whose de one who climbed dahn dur 'n' got 'um?"

"Okay, okay, we can shur um. Let's go make a box-cart."

"Yah. See if you can find a piece-a two-by-four."

"My deddy's got some two-by-four in his shed. I can borrow a piece-a his."

"We still need a box an' some rope, an' a steerin' pin…"

"I see a box. Look over dur."

"Quick! Get it, get it, 'fore dose bies from Smiff Hill see it."

"Yah. Cuz dey'll beat you up 'n' say dey saw it first, you know."

"They better not. I'll 'sook' Barker on 'em."

"Bie, dat dog's not go'n protek you. Hiz too busy chasin' frogs."

"Well, if doze Smiff Hill lot come dis way, you betta run."

"Let's go over my house an' start makin' de cart. Robbie, get dat bicycle wheel over dur. We can use de axel for a steerin' pin."

"Okay."

"We can use my sister's skippin' rope for de steerin'. I know where she hides it."

"Aw right. Errybody meet behine de shed up my house. Llew, you bring some tools."

"Okay. Anybody seen Barker? He-e-r-re, Barker, Barker, Barker! C'mon boy."

The call came just in time. Barker had given up the chase of his elusive quarry in favour of something more appealing. He was nearly knee-deep in mud and contemplating a full mud-bath.

"Last one home's a rotten egg."

We raced home. Barker let me win. I returned the favour by

washing the incriminating evidence off his legs in the leftover laundry water in the tub out back (I think it was leftover).

Dad's tools were the best—a good sharp saw, a professional hammer, an impressive array of screwdrivers, and a great pair of pliers. There was just one problem: Using Dad's tools was strictly taboo. It would rank right up there with sacrilege and treason. I could risk it, but what if I lost or damaged one? Worse, what if one of the other boys claimed one of Dad's tools as his own? Nope, too risky.

Hence, a piece of pipe served as a hammer. A discarded butter knife doubled as a screwdriver, and a nutcracker as pliers. A rusty old saw with half a handle completed the tool kit. With this shoddy collection of makeshift tools, we went to work, crafting for ourselves the sportiest box-cart you ever saw.

I never did have a cart of my own, but I did help to build a couple. That entitled me to alternating turns as driver, pusher, and brake man, which is how I stubbed my toe and lost my toenail for the second time. A second gory description would be needlessly redundant.

There were other accessories that could be added to customise the finished product, like reflectors, mineral bottle caps, carpet, sponge seats and brakes, but these were optional. The main thing was to get the bare bones together and try it out.

Other boys did the same, so we'd meet on Pond Hill for trials.

"Let's see who can range the furthest. Um first."

"Llewellyn, make ya dog behave. He always chases us when we start to run."

"He just wants to play. Can he have a turn, too?"

"Aw right, but tell him behave."

"Okay Barker, no chasing. You hear me? No chasing."

With a burst of power and speed, we launched the first driver, Barker chasing at our heels.

One thing was certain: We were never bored. We were too busy using our imagination while at play, or our ingenuity while learning how to 'fix things.' The Pond offered adventure, amusement, recreation, and more. Really, when I think about it, I can't help but acknowledge some concepts that were ahead of their times.

First, here was recycling at its best, decades before the term came to be in vogue. Very little of what others threw away was wasted. Rather, it was assimilated by someone else who put it to good use, thereby extending its useful life, or the life of another item which would have oth-erwise been discarded.

Secondly, the Pond region represented a vast open space in the middle of the most densely populated part of the Island. It was a lung that breathed life into our com-munity and filtered out the wastes.

Thirdly, many an under-privileged lad learned the rudiments of motor mechan-ics while stripping old bikes and engines, and by trial and error re-assembling them into a working machine. So you might say it offered free, informal, vocational training.

In the fourth instance, it provided an income for some of the more entrepreneurial types who always seemed to find willing buyers for the stuff they retrieved.

Regulars at the dump knew which delivery vehicles brought the best bargains. Some even seemed to know, before the fact, about special shipments of merchandise that could be expected.

One boy we knew managed to get a complete Velo Solex that was in perfect working order right down to having gas in the tank. To this day, we wonder about that bargain and whether some poor unsuspecting bargain hunter left the dump minus the transportation that brought him there.

It's no wonder Barker felt so irresistibly drawn to those environs. Indeed, how could we scold him for his incursions when we, supposedly, his superiors, found such delight there ourselves? He was nothing but a Pond Dog doing what came naturally. What was our excuse?

11

The Pond
from
on high

Five scorching summers and five damp winters passed, or maybe it was six. Time was so abstract to a child of ten. What is more vivid in my recollections is that we moved from Parson's Road to North Hill.

What an improvement! Not only were we away from the main road, but again we had a bigger yard. It spilled over onto a vacant hillside reminiscent of Parker's Hill. Now, instead of being in The Pond, we had a commanding bird's-eye view of everything considered to be part of it, and more.

We could see Government House, the town clock, Gibbs Hill Lighthouse, and all the way to Somerset. A breathtaking panorama, indeed.

Geographically speaking, we now presided over The Pond. We could even look with nostalgia at our former residence and neighbourhood. How happy I am, though, that our humble, happy lifestyle enabled us to look down at, but never down on, The Pond.

If our new neighbourhood atmosphere was dominated by Pond odours, we didn't notice. Fires that burned constantly did

send us occasional whiffs of smoke when the wind shifted to the
west. It would still be years before all that would change, and an
oversized Pond would begin belching its foul breath into the
surrounding air, oozing its pus-like wastes into the surrounding
marshlands, befouling the hallowed sanctuaries therein. But in
those days, the dump was containable. It was certainly tolera-
ble—that is, compared to what it later became.

There was a certain smell, though, that did reign supreme in
at least one nearby sector. It didn't emanate from The Pond

either. Mercifully, we of normal sense of smell lived just out of its range. How Barker endured it, I don't know.

A hundred paces down the rocky path from our house, the first faint whiffs began to tickle our nostrils—just a tease—at about eleven o'clock every morning (except Sundays.) The earliest hints of that scent in the air triggered a marvellous chain reaction between the senses. Taste buds, content since breakfast, awakened. As the smell grew stronger, rumblings like the sound of distant thunder began to echo in hollow bellies.

By a little before noon the scent was torturous. The trickle of digestive juices became a torrent fuelling a mutiny within us. It was the signal for the downing of tools or playthings, and for the pilgrimage of the hungry to begin.

We'd converge, injecting more and more urgency into each stride as we followed the beckoning trail toward the source of the delightful aroma. Two hundred paces and we'd be salivating, bellies churning in anticipation.

Almost there.

The scent hung so heavily in the air, we could chew it. Eager feet shuffled in the waiting area. Through the screen door we could see the huge ovens.

Doors still closed. Not ready yet. Ten more minutes. Might as well be eternity.

Receiving tables and countertops stood cleared and at the ready. By this time the aroma threatened to completely overcome us. Signs of alarm registered on a few unknowing faces.

It's time! I can smell something burning! Not to worry. Just a few oven drippings.

Then—at long last—the object of our pilgrimage! Think of a mouth-watering, tender meat-and-potato filling, wonderfully seasoned. It's then wrapped in a thick pastry, that's baked to golden-brown perfection, and served piping hot. You've just imagined one of Degraff's beef pies, a juicy, self-contained meal—a Pond Dog's delight.

The large, flat baking pans, laden with pies, were transferred from the heat of the ovens into another kind of heat. It was the tumult of a small mob of customers and errand boys all vying for their orders to be filled.

Part of the batch was earmarked for the lunch wagon in town. The rest was made available on a loosely-structured, first-come, first-served basis. Any Pond Dog survival tactics we had acquired were particularly useful at times like these.

All credit to Mr. and Mrs. Degraff and sons; their pies have changed little in thirty-five years, and are as popular today as ever.

I seldom thought of saving a morsel for Barker as a treat. A piece of crust with a trace of filling would have sufficed, I suppose. But as was so often the case, I was too preoccupied with my own indulgence to think of sharing my pie with a dog.

Once, while I was greedily devouring my hearty meal, a sizable chunk broke off, and despite my desperate lunge to salvage it, the ample portion fell toward the ground. To my dismay (and amazement), Barker made a spectacular shoestring catch! (I guess all those years of fly-snatching were practice for this moment.)

I could have cried. In fact, I think I did. Wasn't it poetic justice, though? He always sat so patiently and expectantly, watching me eat, hoping I'd feel inclined to share my treasure, trying to nudge my calloused conscience, then as a last resort willing a piece of whatever I was eating to break off and fall his way. At last there had been a pay-off for his vigilance.

Take that, I scolded myself. You should have shared. That way you could have controlled how much you gave away.

I couldn't blame Barker for what happened. What did I expect him to do? Hand it back? After all, Pond Dogs are opportunists. They seize the moment, because the moments come so few and far between.

From our new, elevated vantage point, we could observe all the goings-on in The Pond. Sprawled before us lay a study in contrasts. We could observe the beehive of activity of the dump, and the idyllic tranquillity of the marsh. Wavy green acres of tall marsh grass belied the stillness of stagnating Pond waters. The density of the Jungle's foliage offset the barrenness of that bleached patch of Desert sand. Our bird's-eye view allowed us to watch Mr. Allen's cows as they grazed undisturbed. We could track a pack of vagabond dogs out on the prowl, or marvel at flocks of fearless scavenger birds descending on the garbage heaps to claim their share of the spoil. We could gaze in astonishment at the perpetual smouldering of the dump fires, and smell the foul odours and acrid smoke if the wind was wrong. We could see those eternal glowing embers get whipped into blazing infernos, with flames that leaped like tongues trying to lick the sky. Best of all on those still, damp mornings, we could look down at the thick blanket of fog that lay trapped in the Pond basin until the warmth of the sun, and a slight breeze, arrived over the crest of the surrounding hills to chase it away. We were further removed, yet at the same time closer to it all.

Barker, like the rest of the family, had to adjust to the new surroundings. Nevertheless, he was not to be denied his Pond escapades. He was born a Pond Dog, and there, beckoning to him, lay his cradle. It was inevitable that he'd find his way down the steep hill, across the main road, over the Desert, and along the verdant banks of the Ditch, to his birthplace. Not even the fence, complete with rustic cedar gate, which Dad and I so proudly built, could deter him.

We built the fence not just to keep Barker in, but to keep other dogs out, and to protect any hapless wayfarer who chanced by. You see, there was a narrow, well-worn footpath which led to our house and provided access to at least two more houses beyond. Evidently, over the years, it had also become a major link in a complicated network of paths forming a short-cut between Friswell's Hill and the foot of Pond Hill. Pedestrian traffic was quite brisk at times, and it was obvious that our presence in the neighbourhood was not going to alter generations of tradition. Barker took exception to these intrusions and confronted passers-by at will. Hence, the fence.

There are no documented cases of his ever biting anyone, but there were scores of close calls after years of trying his hardest. Today, in retrospect, I realise he was only doing his job. He was a watchdog, there to alert his owners to what he saw. That's why he barked so much. He jealously guarded our home, and was prepared to fight to defend his domain from invaders. Therefore, those seemingly senseless attacks on the metreman, the postman, the insurance man, or other visitors, were not so senseless after all.

Please don't misunderstand. Barker wasn't a vicious, ill-tempered animal. On the contrary, he was a wonderful friend and companion, always eager to please, and always happy to see us. He was clever. He was obedient. He was sociable. Together, we could play for hours, or we could hang around and do nothing. He knew how to fetch objects, play tug-o'-war, sit up, lie down, or extend one front paw or the other on command. Then, he wallowed in my too-infrequent praise.

True, there have been times when I have wondered if he did all of these things just to humour me. If he did, he was sure good at faking it, and that would mean he was even cleverer than I thought. He'd deserve an Academy Award for those performances he put on whenever we returned home after being away all day. Sometimes, he'd be so ecstatic we'd have to yell at him, commanding him to be quiet. That was acting? No, I think he was genuinely happy to see us.

As Barker grew older, he resigned himself to the fact The Pond was not as easily accessible as it had been in his youth. His excursions became less frequent, and were confined to within a shrinking radius of the house. People could enter the yard with scarcely a whimper from him. He just couldn't be bothered anymore. He didn't gobble his food down with anything near the same fervor and gusto, and, alas, if I threw a stick or ball, I'd better be prepared to go and fetch it myself. Old Barker was running out of steam.

Someone in the family decided it was time we got another dog—a younger one—presumably to replace the fading old-timer. Not that we were about to bury the old guy, or have him 'put to sleep,' to use that infamous euphemism. That was unthinkable. Let's face it, though, Barker was now twelve or thirteen years old.

Consequently, into our lives came this cute, fuzzy little furball of a puppy. He was mostly black, with a touch of brown. Of course, we all fawned and fussed over the new arrival. So, for a while, Barker had to play second fiddle to an adorable pup.

He seemed to know exactly what was going on, and played his lesser role with all of the graciousness and dignity of an elder statesman. He knew the novelty (and cuteness) would soon wear off. He likely had a good idea what we were in for, too.

We named him Scamp. It soon became apparent he'd more than live up to his name. The dog turned out to be downright silly—part German Shepherd, part idiot.

The only thing I can remember teaching him was how to jump—first, over a broomstick held inches off the ground, eventually, over higher obstacles. Thereafter, he galloped around the yard, leaping over the four-foot-high gate at will. He also attacked the hallowed laundry hanging on the clothesline. As for watchdog qualities, well, let's just say he was no Rin Tin Tin.

It wasn't long before he began to roam. Ultimately, any dog raised in that vicinity and prone to wander, will gravitate to one place, The Pond. One day Scamp did—with near fatal consequences.

Dad was on his weary way home from work, and about to scale the steep hill which led to our candy-pink and white nest. It was the cruellest of hills to encounter at the best of times. After a hard day's labour, however, or a long walk home from town, it was sheer torture to face.

Nevertheless, we tackled that wretched hill dauntlessly, spurning the longer route over Pond Hill as the greater of the two evils. Even with its treacherous pathway, including the dual hairpin turns near the top, the former route offered the more direct approach home. It started as a ramp, graduated to three challenging levels of steps, finally to become a rocky, zigzag footpath that snaked its way upward for what always felt like an eternity. The trip down was just the opposite—a thrill, by comparison.

I loved to go bounding downhill, my feet hardly touching the rock-strewn path, preferring the patchy grass verges instead. I could carve a downward, criss-cross pattern that got me to the bottom in record time. On the other hand, the unbearable burning sensation in the calves and thighs during an attempted record-breaking ascent soon convinced me that the slow trudge was the only sane way to the top.

At any rate, it was somewhere near the foot of this foreboding climb that Dad found the bloodied, limp carcass he recognised as Scamp.

The young, inexperienced dog had been set upon by marauding Pond Dogs. Evidently, they couldn't stand his silliness, and simply refused to tolerate his ignorance of rank and protocol when running with the pack. They beat him up and left him for dead.

He managed to drag his wounded body out of The Pond toward home, but the hill was just too much for him to handle in his weakened state. He lay helpless and panting, his tongue dangling precariously from the side of his mouth, his body punctured by the teeth of his assailants.

Dad carried him home, expecting to have to bury him before the day ended.

I'm sure Barker knew Scamp would have to answer for his folly one day. I imagine he even tried to warn the younger dog, offering him some friendly, fatherly advice, based on his years of experience. But young Scamp was not about to listen to the rantings of some old Pond Dog. Now he was paying the price.

Although we presumed him dead, Mom came to the rescue yet again. Thanks to her, Scamp made a miraculous recovery, although he was never quite the same. From then on, he was nothing but a neurotic dog, permanently scarred emotionally, incapable of being a real pet to anyone. Certainly, he would never be more than a shadow of the dog Barker was. In fact, in my estimation, Barker became all the more remarkable. He had survived all of those years. He knew how to hold his own among the villains of the Pond Dog world. He also knew when to quit.

12

A Pond Dog's lament

Barker made no more pilgrimages to The Pond, except, that is, in his dreams. Occasionally, when I watched him as he slept, his body twitched, his legs feigned a running motion, and his face reflected a peace and contentment that could surely mean but one thing. He was a Pond Dog again, doing what he knew best. He was running with the pack through the muddy marshlands; swimming in the stagnant pond waters; rummaging through the trash for tasty, albeit slightly spoiled, tidbits. Once more he was rolling deliriously in some foul-smelling heap of unidentifiable gunk, chasing giant frogs or pond rats—and catching them! I'm not quite sure, but I think at such times I saw him smile.

He was my pal, my confidante, my playmate. With him I could pout, cry, laugh, pretend, or be myself. He didn't mind. We'd grown up together.

He'd seen me get my first bicycle, and later, my first motorised bike—a Mobylette. He watched with curiosity as I stripped the old second-hand moped, scraped and sanded the creamy yellow paint off, primed it, re-painted it (navy blue and grey), and proudly reassembled it in anticipation of my reaching the legal riding age. He was content to watch as I dawdled for hours tinkering with that rickety bike.

He witnessed the arrival of my first brand new Mobylette, too, and never complained at being ignored in favour of the shiny new toy. He even saw us get our first family car, a 1967 Volkswagen Beetle. When I sneaked home late at night and eased down the hill and into the yard, he co-operated splendidly by not barking. He read the situation perfectly. Why disturb my sleeping parents and sisters unnecessarily? He made not a whimper. I think I reminded him of his youthful Pond Dog days.

All too soon, I had reached the age of twenty. Barker was about sixteen. That's about one-hundred-and-twelve in dog years, they say. He had grown visibly old. The hairs around his snout had turned grey, like the stubble on the face of an old man. His eyes, devoid of their youthful lustre, looked dim. Pond flies could dance in his dish, or land right on his nose with impunity. And his arthritic limbs carried him only with difficulty. The once energetic wagging of his tail was reduced to a few strained gestures of the hindquarters that told us the thought was still there. The grand old man had reached the limit of his days. He may have been nothin' but a Pond Dog, but when he died, I cried for him as if I'd lost a brother. And in many ways I had. For having come from the same area and having lived the same experiences, was I not really a Pond Dog too?

Pond Dogs are a special breed—not given to the pampered life of their elitist, purebred cousins. Indeed, if the truth be known, they are most often disowned by the fairer breeds. They are the canine "untouchables"—the rogues of dogdom, who haunt the vilest of places and dine on the unthinkable. Driven by primordial instincts, they run in blood-thirsty packs, wreaking havoc and mayhem, in unabashed celebration. Impervious to cold, and rain, and heat alike, they mock the elements, their coarse, hardened exteriors already tempered for one thing: Survival.

Lowly Pond Dogs aren't supposed to be pets, it's said. They're "unaccustomed to domesticity," best suited to the wilds, where dog-eat-dog is the familiar creed. How could they love or be loved?

Nevertheless the irony was, as many a child from the back of town knew, Pond Dogs made wonderful pets. They were as loving, playful, loyal, friendly and noble as any dog that is wanted and cared for. What families in the Pond area offered helpless, homeless pups was a life beyond the flies, the rats and the stench—something more than the all-night binges of violence and the plundering of someone's livestock. It was a path away from the dark, seamy side of Pond life.

Barker successfully made the transition without losing his identity. For me, he helped explode the myths about Pond Dogs. He was living proof that, whether Pond Dog or pedigree, the measure of what one is comes from deep within, and not from one's geographical origin.

Who would have thought that such a poignant, lifelong lesson could be taught by a simple Pond Dog?

APPENDIX
YOU KNOW YOU'RE A POND DOG IF...

1. You're from Parson's Road.
2. You're from Pond Hill, North Hill, or Friswell's Hill.
3. You're from Marsh Folly or Government Gate.
4. Ya from "rahn de Curve."
5. Ya from de Smiff Hill errea.
6. You know what #5 means.
7. You've ever lived within view, earshot, or smelling range of the Pembroke Dump.
8. You attended Central School.
9. Something inside you can't resist the rhythm of the Gombeys.
10. You've ever "shopped for bargains" at the dump.
11. You've ever taken trash to the dump and *not* returned empty-handed.
12. You ever played in, hid in, or "got licks" for hanging around The Pond.
13. You've ever successfully jumped The Ditch.
14 You've ever fallen (or been pushed) in.
15. The Desert was ever your softball team's home ground.
16. You've ever ridden a box-cart down Pond Hill.
17. You've ever ridden a box-cart down Pond Hill *with no brakes*.

18. You used to play football in the tall grass on the corner of Glebe and Parson's where the playground is now.

19. You love Degraff's beef pies.

20. You used to play tennis at the Unity Tennis Court.

21.You refuse(d) to be caught dead in tennis whites.

22. People used to make fun of you if you dared to do so.

23. You know what to do when you're the passenger on a bicycle with no seat.

24. You know what to do when you're the *rider* on a bicycle with no seat.

25. You know what to do when you're the rider or passenger on a bike with no brakes.

26. You've ever played hooky from school and spent the day in The Pond.

27. You've ever played hooky from *work* and spent the day in The Pond.

28. You've ever wanted to play hooky from *life* and spend the day in The Pond.

29. Your first bike was built from, or enhanced by, parts scavenged from the dump.

30. You used to run barefooted on the hot, tarred roads without burning your feet.

31. You used to run barefooted on the roads before they were tarred.

32. You used to run barefooted before there were roads!

33. You remember "knockers."

34. The house you lived in had an outhouse.

35. Your neighbours had an outhouse.

36. You were on Mr. Ford's paper route.

37. You could hear Mr. Goater whistling as he passed your house.

38. You used to hitch a ride on the tailgate of Mr. Dane's horse-drawn wagon.

39. You ever attempted to take a short-cut through his farmyard.

40. You were ever chased by his geese.

41. They ever caught you!

42. You were fast enough to outrun them!

43. You know what bongies, warties, smallies and shooties are, and what they are used for.

44. You remember Mrs. Hutchinson balancing bundles on her head as she walked along Parson's Road.

45. Your night-time entertainment was watching the dump fires burn.

46. You know what it's like to inhale the smoke or stench from The Pond day after day after day.

47. Old-timers from that area still recognise you—or, at least, know (and can tell you) who your family is.

48. Fond memories and warm feelings of nostalgia come flooding back whenever you're in the vicinity of The Pond.

49. You see a scruffy, old mongrel and feel a strange and instant kinship with him.

50. Any of the foregoing has touched a familiar chord.